# When All Seems Fading

# When All Seems Fading

E. C. Nakeli

King's Word Publishing

© 2016 by E.C. Nakeli

1st publication in 2008

2nd publication by King's Word Publication, 2016

For your questions and publishing needs, write to:

    E.C. Nakeli
    40 S Church st
    Westminster, MD 21157
    E-mail: *ecnakeli@yahoo.com*

Printed in the United States of America

All rights reserved. No part of this publication may be reproduced, stored in a retrieval systems, or transmitted in ay form or by any means— for example, electronic, photocopy, recording—without the prior written permission of the publisher. The only exception is brief quotations in printed reviews.

E.C. Nakeli

To contact the author, write to:

    E.C. Nakeli
    40 S Church st
    Westminster, MD 21157
    E-mail: *ecnakeli@yahoo.com*

When All Seems Fading/ E.C. Nakeli

ISBN: 978-1-945055-01-0

    Unless otherwise indicated, Scriptures references are from
    THE HOLY BIBLE, NEW INTERNATIONAL VERSION®, NIV®
    Copyright © 1973, 1978, 1984, 2011 by Biblica, Inc™
    Used by permission. All rights reserved worlwide.

Cover Design: Zach Essama

## Table of Contents

Chapter 1: God's Promises ..................................................................1
Chapter 2: The Certainty of His Promise ............................................9
Chapter 3: The Testing of Your Faith ................................................15
Chapter 4: The Testing of Your Integrity ..........................................25
Chapter 5: The Testing of The Promise ............................................31
Chapter 6: When You Fell Like Giving Up .......................................37
Chapter 7: When You Have Given Up ..............................................45
Chapter 8: The Power of Obedience .................................................51
Chapter 9: The Power of Surrending .................................................59
Chapter 10: The Power of Tears .........................................................63
Chapter 11: The Power of the Altar ...................................................67
Chapter 12: Don't Get It All Wrong, God Is Not Indifferent ...........71
Chapter 13: Keep Holding On ...........................................................77
Chapter 14: Overcoming Loneliness ..................................................87
Chapter 15: When God Breaks Into Your World .............................93
Chapter 16: Teaching You Dependence .............................................99
Chapter 17: Your Reward Shall Come .............................................107
In Closing ...........................................................................................159

# CHAPTER 1

## God's Promises

Now, the whole Bible is full of God's promises, and many a times, believers tend to claim them thinking all that is needed is faith, and that just any promise can be claimed. To claim any promise, we need to understand certain underlying principles. This is the purpose of the first chapter of this book.

**What then is a promise?**

*"A promise is an assurance given by one person to another, that the former will or will not do a specific act"* Funk and Wagnals.

From this simple definition, we can understand that not every statement is a promise, even if it makes an offer.

**Essential factors of a promise**

For any statement to be qualified as a promise there must be the following:

1. A *promisor*: This is the person who makes a promise. It can be one nation to another, a younger person to an older one and vice versa, it can be a boss to a subordinate or the other way round. Whatever the case, there must be a promisor, the one who gives his word.

2. A *promisee*: This is the one to whom the promise is made. He is the one who rightfully has to expect from his promisor whatever was promised.
3. Statement of Promise: It does not suffice for there to be a *promisor* and a *promisee*. There must also be the statement of promise, for the same *promisor* and *promisee* can have different promises depending on the statement of the promise.
4. The Conditions surrounding the Promise: These include the circumstances that surround both the *promisor* and the *promisee* at the time of the promise. It includes the terms of the promise, both the pre and post conditions of fulfilment.
5. The time frame: There may or may not be a specific time frame for every promise. However, most often there is a time frame within which the promise is valid and within which the *promisor* can be held accountable by the *promisee*.

Let me give some examples to make my point very clear as to the essential nature of each of the factors above. Suppose Mary walks into a room and reads on the wall *"I'll give you a new Bible"*. That's all she reads. Now the author of that statement is unknown, the object of the statement is not specified. All there is a subject. Can Mary call that a promise? Can she claim it as a promise? No, no *promisee*, such a statement can never be considered a promise. Now suppose Mary knows the author of that statement. Can she hold him accountable for the statement? The answer surely is a big no! Why? Because there is no *promisee*! Mary has not been specified as the object of the promise.

Again, suppose the statement read, *"I will give you a new Bible, Mary"* Surely this kind of statement specifies a *promisee*, but there is no *promisor*, so the *promisee* cannot hold anyone accountable for such a statement. Let us suppose that the author of the statement is known and Mary moves up to him and says, *"You just promised me a new Bible"* and he says, *"Yeah I did"*. Mary may then ask, under what conditions? If there are any he may go ahead and give her the conditions or he may just say there are no conditions. If Mary leaves at this point rejoicing that she has been promised a new Bible, then I tell you, she might as well wait until she dies without receiving one. Why? Because there was no time frame given! The time of fulfilment was left only at the promisor's discretion.

You now see the need for each of the factors above for a promise to be completely defined. With this in mind, we will now move on to the next stage.

## Kinds of Promises

There are three major classes of promises and two subclasses to look at.

### 1. Conditional Promises:

These are promises with preconditions clearly tied to them. For such a promise to be fulfilled, all the preconditions must be fulfilled, without which the *promisee* has no right to claim the promise, for example, God's promise to His people in 2 Chronicles 7:14. Its fulfilment depends largely on the *promisee*.

> *"...If my people, who are called by my name, will humble themselves and pray and seek my face and turn from their wicked ways, then will I hear from heaven and will forgive their sin and will heal their land."*
> (2 Chronicles 7:14)

This is a promise of forgiveness and healing on God's people, but it is clearly tied to the following preconditions

People concerned must be God's people called by His name,

- They must humble themselves;
- They must pray;
- They must seek the Lord's face;
- They must turn from their wicked ways.

Must be met otherwise no forgiveness and healing should be expected. A people may fulfil four of the above but without the fifth, they have no mandate to claim forgiveness and healing.

## 2. Absolute Promises:

These are promises with no preconditions. Such promises depend largely on the promisor and often take the form of an oath. The *promisee* has virtually no part to play but to expect and receive the fulfilment of the promise. What counts here is the integrity of the promisor; as long as the promisor can be trusted then the *promisee* can wait with eager expectation to see the promise fulfilled.

An example of such a promise is God's promise of a son to Abram.

> "*But Abram said, "O Sovereign LORD, what can you give me since I remain childless and the one who will inherit my estate is Eliezer of Damascus?" And Abram said, "You have given me no children; so a servant in my household will be my heir." Then the word of the LORD came to him: "This man will not be your heir, but a son coming from your own body will be your heir." He took him outside and said, "Look up at the heavens and count the stars--if indeed you can count them." Then he said to him, "So shall your offspring be*" (Genesis 15:2-5).

The only part Abram had in this promise is that he was the *promisee*. Other than that all he had to do was to believe God, which at some point he failed to, but because it was an absolute promise God fulfilled His Word.

## 3. Absolute - Conditional Promises:

These promises are in two phases: one conditional and the other absolute. Here the promisor promises to do something, after which the *promisee* has to do something for the last part of the deal to be fulfilled. Such promises take the form of covenants. An example of such a promise is God's promise to Abram about his descendants inheriting the Land.

> "*When Abram was ninety-nine years old, the LORD appeared to him and said, 'I am God Almighty; walk before me and be blameless. I will confirm my covenant between me and you and will greatly increase your numbers.'*

> *Abram fell facedown, and God said to him, 'As for me, this is my covenant with you: You will be the father of many nations. No longer will you be called Abram; your name will be Abraham, for I have made you a father of many nations. I will make you very fruitful; I will make nations of you, and kings will come from you. I will establish my covenant as an everlasting covenant between me and you and your descendants after you for the generations to come, to be your God and the God of your descendants after you. The whole land of Canaan, where you are now an alien, I will give as an everlasting possession to you and your descendants after you; and I will be their God.' Then God said to Abraham, 'As for you, you must keep my covenant, you and your descendants after you for the generations to come. This is my covenant with you and your descendants after you, the covenant you are to keep: Every male among you shall be circumcised. You are to undergo circumcision, and it will be the sign of the covenant between me and you. For the generations to come every male among you who is eight days old must be circumcised, including those born in your household or bought with money from a foreigner--those who are not your offspring. Whether born in your household or bought with your money, they must be circumcised. My covenant in your flesh is to be an everlasting covenant.'*
> "*Then God said, 'Yes, but your wife Sarah will bear you a son, and you will call him Isaac. I will establish my covenant with him as an everlasting covenant for his descendants after him*'" (Genesis 17: 1-13, 19).

The first part of this promise is absolute, That of God giving Abram a descendant, a son from his own loins. The second part is conditional: Abram circumcising the males of his household and naming his son Isaac when he was born. Abram's fulfilment of these conditions had to ensure the continuation of the covenant and the eventual possession of the land by his descendants.

Having brought out these three categories of promises, there's one more thing I'll like us to look at; the time factor.

Each of the above categories of promise can be time bounded or time-unbounded. God sets a time limit for some promises, which I call time-bounded promises, no matter the category.

For example God's promise to Jehu about the throne of Israel!

> "*The LORD said to Jehu, 'Because you have done well in accomplishing what is right in my eyes and have done to the house of Ahab all I had in mind to do, your descendants will sit on the throne of Israel to the fourth generation'*" (2 Kings 10:30).

The time limit of God's promise to Jehu about the throne was the fourth generation and this promise was fulfilled. It would have been foolish for any descendant of Jehu after the fourth generation to claim any right to the throne of Israel.

> "*So the word of the Lord spoken to Jehu was fulfilled: 'your descendant will sit on the throne of Israel to the fourth generation'*" (2 Kings 15:12).

There are also everlasting promises, i.e. they have no time limit. An example is God's promise to David about the throne. Such a promise was forever.

> "*'I declare to you that the LORD will build a house for you: When your days are over and you go to be with your fathers, I will raise up your offspring to succeed you, one of your own sons, and I will establish his kingdom. He is the one who will build a house for me, and I will establish his throne forever. I will be his father, and he will be my son. I will never take my love away from him, as I took it away from your predecessor. I will set him over my house and my kingdom forever; his throne will be established forever'*" (1 Chronicles 17:10b-14).

Another example is God's promise to His Son about His Priesthood.

> "*No one takes this honor upon himself; he must be called by God, just as Aaron was. ⁵So Christ also did not take upon himself the glory of becoming a high priest. But God said to him, "You are my Son; today I have become your Father." ⁶And he says in another place, "You are a priest forever, in the order of Melchizedek"*" (Hebrews 5:4-6).

So whatever the category a promise may belong to, let us understand the time factor before setting out to claim the promise.

## The Purpose of His Promise

God does not make promises to His children to please them or to make them glory in themselves. Every promise of God is tied to His plan and purpose for this universe. God makes no promise contrary to His eternal plan and purpose. If this is so then we can trust Him and must trust Him to fulfil that which He has promised. Before you claim any of God's promises, all things taken into consideration you should ask yourself *"how the fulfilment of that promise in your life will foster God's plan for you as an individual and for mankind as a whole?"*

God's promises are never meant to foster the selfish ambitions and motives of puny man, though man certainly benefits from them. No matter what the promise is, the overall purpose is His eternal plan and purpose which are surely coming to fulfilment in these last days.

## Why God does what He does?

You and I need not necessarily understand how God does what He does, but at least the Bible lets us Know why He does what He does.

> *"I know that everything God does will endure forever; nothing can be added to it and nothing taken from it. God does it so that men will revere him"* (Ecclesiates 3:14).

### 1. Durability.

The word *"endure"* here talks of the ability to resist and stay in the best condition with respect to time and circumstances. He alone knows the circumstances which will surround you and His promise to you hundreds of years from now. He alone knows the needs that will arise hundreds of years from now.

## 2. What God does is final

God is the greatest power, the highest authority in this whole-wide universe. He alone is infinitely wise. He places His seal on what He says and does, therefore no one can change them whether by addition or by subtraction. No one can reverse whatever God does (See also Isaiah 43:13).

## 3. God does everything to reveal His glory.

God's plan is that all creation may come to revere Him as God. The whole prophecy in Ezekiel is filled with the phrase *"Then they will know that I am the Lord"*.

His eternal purpose is that man may behold His glory and turn back to Him. The Bible says,

> *"His intent was that now, through the church, the manifold wisdom of God should be made known to the rulers and authorities in the heavenly realms, and according to his eternal purpose which he accomplished in Christ Jesus our Lord"* (Ephesians 3:10-11).

## 4. He alone knows the best time for everything.

> *"There is a time for everything, and a season for every activity under heaven"*
> *"He has made everything beautiful in its time"* (Ecclesiastes 3:1,11a).

There's a time interval within which anything particular has to be accomplished in order for there to be greatest results. God alone knows what should be done and when. Why? **"Because He has made everything beautiful in its own time"**. Out of its time it becomes ugly and without attraction. This places a responsibility on the one to whom the promise is given to discern or understand the time of the promise.

# CHAPTER 2

## The Certainty of His Promise

No matter the category of the promise, no matter the time factor, as long as it is a promise from God, then such a promise will surely come to fulfilment. Why?

*"God is not a man, that he should lie, nor a son of man, that he should change his mind. Does he speak and then not act? Does he promise and not fulfil?"* (Number 23:19)

**God is Truth and He cannot lie:**

If the promise were from a man, one can think that such a promise cannot be true, but because it is from God, and God by His very nature is the Truth, what He says will surely come to fulfilment. The Bible says, *"God is light and in Him there is no darkness"*. About Israel, it is said, by God's word *"Not one of all the LORD'S good promises to the house of Israel failed; everyone was fulfilled"* (Joshua 21:45).

*"Praise be to the LORD, who has given rest to His people Israel just as He promised. Not one word has failed of all the good promises He gave through His servant Moses"* (1 Kings 8:56).

God does not change His mind about the good He promises. You know often as humans we make up our mind at one moment and change it at some other, especially when it comes to doing people favours. Often, this change of mind is as a result of the person's attitude toward us or the things which affect us within the period of our intended favour. Not so with God. When He has given a promise, His Word, He does not change His mind; this will mean changing His Word. He says,

> *"I will not violate my covenant or alter what my lips have uttered"*
> *"If his sons forsake my law and do not follow my statutes, if they violate my decrees and fail to keep my commands, I will punish their sin with the rod, their iniquity with flogging; but I will not take my love from him, nor will I ever betray my faithfulness. I will not violate my covenant or alter what my lips have uttered. Once for all, I have sworn by my holiness—and I will not lie to David -that his line will continue forever and his throne endure before me like the sun; it will be established forever like the moon, the faithful witness in the sky"* (Psalm 89:30-37).

**God fulfils His promises.**

Every promise God has made, He will fulfil. Even as He has said again and again in time past, He is doing it now and will continue to do it. He says in His eternal Word *"For no matter how many promises God has made, they are 'yes' in Christ"* (2 Corinthians 1:20a).

Remember we said God's promises to individuals and to the church are tied to His eternal plan and purpose for all creation. The same commitment God has to His eternal plan is the same commitment He has to every promise of His. Just as nothing, absolutely nothing, can thwart His purpose, nothing, absolutely nothing can destroy any promise of His. Did He not ask, *"For the LORD Almighty Has purposed, and who can thwart Him? His hand is stretched out, and who can turn it back?"* (Isaiah 14: 27). To these questions the answer is no one, absolutely no one. For *"there is no one holy like the LORD; there is no one besides you; there is no Rock like our God"* (1 Samuel 2:2).

And

> *"Who among the gods is like you, O LORD? Who is like you - majestic in holiness, awesome in glory, working wonders?"* (Exodus 15:11)

Has not God said *"Surely, as I have planned, so it will be, and as I have purposed, so it will stand"* (Isaiah 14:24)?

When I first meditated on this verse, I wrote down the following:

God's purpose for my life will stand. His plans for my life will come to pass. Everything He wrote about me in His book will be realized. The LORD Almighty is committed to realizing His plans and purposes for me as an individual. All I need to do is to be sure that this or that is God's plan and purpose for me and take sides with God through:

1. **Consecration:**

Sanctification and availability. Availability to God and His servants.

2. **Obedience to the Word and the Voice of God.**

I need not fear anything; whatever is God's purpose for my life must surely come to fulfilment.

1. Thank You LORD because your plans and purposes for my life concerning marriage will surely come to pass
2. Thank you LORD because your plans and purpose for my life concerning studies will come to pass
3. Thank you LORD because you plans and purposes for my life concerning ministry will surely come to pass.
4. Thank you LORD because your plans and purposes for my life concerning vocation will surely come to pass.
5. Thank you LORD because your plans and purposes for my life concerning finance will surely come to pass

6. Thank you LORD because your plans and purposes for my life concerning health will surely come to pass.

Now for a moment let's see how this promise was certain in Abraham's life.

> *"Now the LORD was gracious to Sarah as he had said, and the LORD did for Sarah what he had promised. Sarah became pregnant and bore a son to Abraham in his old age, at the very time God had promised him. Abraham gave the name Isaac to the son Sarah bore him. When his son Isaac was eight days old, Abraham circumcised him, as God commanded him. Abraham was a hundred years old when his son Isaac was born to him"* (Genesis 21:1-5).

As we said before, whatever God has said that He will do and whatever He has promised, that He will fulfil. As we saw, this was an absolute promise and it had nothing to do with Sarah. In spite of her attitude of gross unbelief God went ahead to do as He had promised. Again I say we are talking of Sarah who doubted God's word, one who laughed and lied she didn't.

> *"Then the LORD said, 'I will surely return to you about this time next year, and Sarah your wife will have a son.' Now Sarah was listening at the entrance to the tent, which was behind him. Abraham and Sarah were already old and well advanced in years, and Sarah was past the age of childbearing. So Sarah laughed to herself as she thought, 'After I am worn out and my master is old, will I now have this pleasure?' Then the LORD said to Abraham, 'Why did Sarah laugh and say, "Will I really have a child, now that I am old?" Is anything too hard for the LORD? I will return to you at the appointed time next year and Sarah will have a son.' Sarah was afraid, so she lied and said, 'I did not laugh.' But he said, 'Yes, you did laugh.'"* (Genesis 18:10-15).

What am I trying to bring out?

God mostly overlooks our failures and weaknesses in faith to work out everything according to His eternal plans and purpose. In spite of your weaknesses the sovereign LORD will bring about His every promise. Well, the promise was not to Sarah but to Abraham the man of faith who *"believed God and it*

*The Certainty of His Promise*

*was credited to him as righteousness"*. Yes it is the same Abraham whose faith had dwindled, who now doubted God's very word, one who laughed and asked questions. Yes we are talking about an Abraham who couldn't see beyond Ishmael, contented with his own failure.

> *"Abraham fell face down; he laughed and said to himself, 'will a son be born to a man a hundred years old? Will Sarah bear a child at the age of ninety?' And Abraham said to God, 'if only Ishmael might live under your blessing!'"* (Genesis 17:17-18)

God saw Isaac while Abraham saw Ishmael. God saw the future to which His promise to Abraham was tied but all what Abraham could see was the now and immediate. He saw only his failures and could not imagine he would rise beyond his failures, more so as the product of his failure stood right before him. It is time to lift up your eyes and look into the future God is pointing to you. Rise and embrace your Isaac, leaving behind your Ishmael. What are the Ishmaels you have brought into your life as a result of impatience? God is asking you to look beyond them. Do not insist for Him to bless your Ishmael but go on for your Isaac. Hallelujah.

## The timing of the promise

> *"Sarah became pregnant and bore a son to Abraham in his old age, at the very time God had promised him."*

Initially when the promise was given to Abraham in chapter 15, there was no time stated for its fulfilment. Further in chapter 17 when God reinstated the promise, there was no time stated for its fulfilment. What we must know is that, ones there is no time given for the fulfilment of a promise, all we need to do is trust in the one who gave the promise, rather than running out of patience to bring to existence Ishmaels who later can only become thorns to our flesh.

In chapter 18, *"...the LORD said, 'I will surely return to you about this time next year, and Sarah your wife will have a son.'"* This was the second confirmation of the same promise but this time around the time of fulfilment is clearly stated. Abraham had every right and every reason to have expected one year later, the fulfilment of this promise. God had given them a time limit and by His faithfulness we read *"Sarah became pregnant and bore a son to Abraham in his old age, at the very time God had promised him"*. Won't you lift up your hands and bless the LORD for being so faithful? *"At the very time God had promised him"* God cannot fail in His promises, all we need to do is understand the intended time of fulfilment. God is never late; He is a God who keeps to time.

The problem with us is that we do not understand the time for which God has made a promise and way too often we get anxious and in this anxiety to see the promise fulfilled we think time is running out. God is not an opportunist such that circumstances will force Him to act. He creates the situations to suit His program for our individual lives. All we need is expectancy and not anxiety. True expectancy is void of anxiety and when anxiety steps in, we stop expecting and start seeking to bring about the fulfilment using our own schemes and manipulations. We give Him the glory, as He can always and does always transcend our failures and shortcomings to bring about a greater purpose. Praise Him whose love and mercies endure forever!

# CHAPTER 3

## The Testing of Your Faith

Without proper understanding of a promise, no matter how much faith we profess, we soon realize our faith has dwindled and left us wanting in the test of time. This was exactly the case of Abraham, the father of faith. After God's command to Abraham and the promise which followed, the Bible says: *"So Abram left, as the LORD had told him"* (Genesis 12:4a). The writer of Hebrews lets us know this was an act of faith; his settling in Canaan was an act of faith.

> *"By faith Abraham, when called to go to a place he would later receive as his inheritance, obeyed and went, even though he did not know where he was going. By faith he made his home in the Promised Land like a stranger in a foreign country; he lived in tents, as did Isaac and Jacob, who were heirs with him of the same promise. For he was looking forward to the city with foundations, whose architect and builder is God"* (Hebrew 11:8-10).

When the promise was reiterated in Genesis 15, the Bible says *"Abram believed God and He credited it to him as righteousness."* (Genesis 15:6) This promise was later sealed with a sacrifice and a covenant with God Most High. The next chapter has a sad beginning of Abram, agreeing with his wife (who was ignorant at the time of the promise) to act against the promise of God. The first test of our faith with respect to the promise will come as pressure from our immediate environment. It usually will come from those we love and cherish but who are ignorant of the promise given to us. It is your responsibility to hold unto God's promise for you. Do not expect everyone and everything to act in favour of His promise for your life. Often we seem to have faith that moves mountains but stumble over anthills. God help us!

In Genesis 17:17, the Bible says *"Abraham fell face down, he laughed and said to himself, 'Will a son be born to a man a hundred years old? Will Sarah bear a child at the age of ninety?'"*

In claiming the promises of God we trust God's mercy and faithfulness and not our faith. If all Abraham relied on was his faith, which initially looked so strong but waned over the years, then there would be no Israel and consequently no Messiah. At the time the promise was first given, Abraham, combined his faith with the physical evidences, for at this time he was just seventy five and Sarah was just sixty-five and it was just naturally possible for them to still bring forth a child. The *"delay"* was to bring all physical possibilities to naught, so his faith could rest not on the physical but on the invisible. So our faith will secondly be tested by the time factor and thirdly by the *"impossibilities"*.

Another vivid example of the testing of our faith can be seen in the New Testament, in the life of Zechariah the priest. Now take a look at the narrative:

> *"'For he will be great in the sight of the Lord. He is never to take wine or other fermented drink, and he will be filled with the Holy Spirit even from birth. Many of the people of Israel will he bring back to the Lord their God. And he will go on before the Lord, in the spirit and power of Elijah, to turn the hearts of the fathers to their children and the disobedient to the wisdom of the righteous—to make ready a people prepared for the Lord.' Zechariah asked the angel, 'How can I be sure of this? I am an old man and my wife is well along in years.' The angel answered, 'I am Gabriel. I stand in the presence of God, and I have been sent to speak to you and to tell you this good news. And now you will be silent and not able to speak until the day this happens, because you did not believe my words, which will come true at*

*their proper time.' Meanwhile, the people were waiting for Zechariah and wondering why he stayed so long in the temple. When he came out, he could not speak to them. They realized he had seen a vision in the temple, for he kept making signs to them but remained unable to speak."* (Luke 1:15-22)

Here you find a couple who were,

1. Upright in the sight of God
2. Observing the commands and regulations blamelessly
3. Childless
4. Both well on in years.

A few lessons to be drawn here: uprightness in the sight of God does not mean exclusion from pain and suffering. God at times temporarily withholds answers to the prayers of the upright. This is done so that something greater may be given at the proper time, so that your needs, God's need and the need of the world may be met. There are prayers that God will answer only when all evidence for a solution is gone. But you ask, *"How does all this relate to the testing of our faith?"*

Surely, as a priest, Zechariah knew of God's promise to answer prayers. Yet this man of God had given up any hope to receive a response to their prayer. His faith had failed the test of time but God in His sovereignty decided to overlook his weakness to achieve a greater purpose.

## Lessons to note

- No one should make prayers for which he will not trust God to answer.
- There is no excuse to disbelieve God even when there are clear and legitimate evidences against His promise.
- Unbelief and lack of trust are shear opposition to God, and to oppose God is to court His judgment.
- Promises made come true at the *"proper time"*; prayers are answered at the *"proper time"*. No amount of worry or anxiety can push God to fulfil His word at an improper time.

- It is sin against God to compare His word with evidences. Any attempt to put God's word on a scale balance with evidences is failure because the evidences will invariably be weightier.
- God in His love and faithfulness will still fulfil His promises in spite of unbelief. God cannot be limited, not even by unbelief.
- You need not be committed to God's will only, but also to the proper time, hence labour to be led by the Spirit into His proper time.

**Peter and the promise**

Take a look at the promise of our LORD Jesus Christ to Peter:

> *"When Jesus came to the region of Caesarea Philippi, he asked his disciples, 'Who do people say the Son of Man is?' They replied, 'Some say John the Baptist; others say Elijah; and still others, Jeremiah or one of the prophets.' 'But what about you?' he asked. 'Who do you say I am?' Simon Peter answered, 'You are the Christ, the Son of the living God.' Jesus replied, 'Blessed are you, Simon son of Jonah, for this was not revealed to you by man, but by my Father in heaven. And I tell you that you are Peter, and on this rock I will build my church, and the gates of Hades will not overcome it. I will give you the keys of the kingdom of heaven; whatever you bind on earth will be bound in heaven, and whatever you loose on earth will be loosed in heaven'"* (Matthew 16:13-19).

The following promises were made to Peter in this passage.

1. He was to be the rock on which Christ was going to build His church
2. Peter was to be given the keys of the Kingdom
3. Whatever Peter bound on earth would be bound in Heaven
4. Whatever Peter loosed on earth would be loosed in Heaven.

Such a promise could have made Peter see himself as an invincible, impeccable creature on which even God can rely. A rock represents strength, firmness and reliability. If Christ could address Peter as a rock then we can say Peter was strong enough to face any situation, he could stand firm no matter what might have challenged his allegiance to the Christ. He could be reliable enough to carry on whatever was entrusted to him. From this time on we could have expected that Peter would experience no failure, that he would overcome every obstacle, for he had been declared a rock. Permit me bring out some situations in Peter's life *"when all seemed fading"*.

## Fallen Peter

I presume that according to Peter's understanding of God's promise, he had been set apart from the other disciples. Even if they failed he, the rock, was now infallible and so boldly and confidently Peter could declare against the prediction of Christ "Even if all fall away on account of You, I never will" (Matthew 26:33). To paraphrase the above statement,

> *"All the others can betray You, Jesus, but not me"*
> *"All the others can abandon the cause but not me"*
> *"Master, you can trust me, even if you wouldn't trust the others"*.

As if that was not enough, Peter in his zeal for the LORD, declared himself the first martyr–to-be on behalf of Christ. *"Even if I have to die with You, I will never disown you"* (Matthew 26:35).

Could such zeal and declaration in the flesh stand the test of time and changing circumstances?

> *"Then Jesus told them, 'This very night you will all fall away on account of me, for it is written: "I will strike the shepherd, and the sheep of the flock will be scattered." But after I have risen, I will go ahead of you into Galilee.' Peter replied, 'Even if all fall away on account of you, I never will.' 'I tell you the truth,' Jesus answered, 'This very night, before the rooster crows, you will disown me three times.' But Peter declared, 'Even if I have to die with you, I will never disown you.' And all the other disciples said the same."*
> (Matthew 26: 31-35)

Here is the one who, a few verses before, had pledged a never failing allegiance to the Master, one who promised to stand tall when all others were falling; we find him denying his Master three consecutive times, once in the presence of an unarmed servant girl (see Matthew 26:69-75). Peter who drew out a sword and stroke someone's ear when the *"weak disciples"* were present refused to own his master when he, the rock, was all alone.

No matter how strong you are, you need someone to hold your hand; someone to give you courage in times of need, no matter how weak that one may seem. Note that each time Peter disowned the LORD, he moved further away from His presence. From the courtyard to the gateway to the outside! But you say, *"Well I have never denied the Savior"*. Well by your compromises with the world in its standards and values, ways and interests have you not disowned Him? By your pursuits and priorities have you not disowned Him? By your style of dressing, your choice of music and movie have you not betrayed Him?

If you read John's account of this event, you will realize doors had to be opened for Peter to get in. Did Peter know such testing awaited him? Sometimes, doors will be opened for you to go in and face trials, temptations and severe testing. Doors will be opened into suffering and persecution and interrogation about the sincerity of your allegiance to the LORD. There is one great lesson we should learn from this event, even if all the others escape your grasp labour to get this one: Peter had a listening ear to hear the crow of the cock and understand its implications.

As a believer you should develop a listening ear to nature and the environment. You should learn to understand the message each carries across. God has placed His cocks of nature around us, not to spy on us but to crow when need be so as to remind us of our allegiance to Him, and the predictions and promises of Christ our LORD. Even with your determination to follow with all courage and boldness, there will be trials in the face of which you might be tempted to deny the Savior but if you listen to the voice of God in that circumstance and heed His warning, things will be different.Should you fail in the face of trials, never fail to recognize the crow of the cock–a call to heart-rending repentance and brokenness. I do not know how far you have gone in your compromise. I do not know how close you are to the fire lit by the world so that you may keep warm. I do not know how many times and how far you have gone in your compromises. I do not know before whom and for what reason you've disowned Him. You thought in your compromises things would become better, but instead they seem to fade the more. You did not mean it to reach the extent to which you have gone. You look back at when it all started and regret you ever got involved. At such a moment as this, take your eyes from yourself and from the environment and like Peter look up to the face of the Savior, remember His words to you and ask for forgiveness. His arms are open wide to receive you if you truly repent and abandon your compromises. God is faithful!

## Backslidden Peter

> *"'I'm going out to fish,' Simon Peter told them, and they said, 'We'll go with you.' So they went out and got into the boat, but that night they caught nothing."* (John 21:3)

Surely you and I know that at the call of Peter, the LORD changed his profession from a *"fisher of fish"* to a fisher of men (see Matthew 4: 18-20, Mark 1:16-17, Luke 5:10).

Peter had received a commission from the LORD and it is on the basis of this commission that the promise was given to Peter. For more than three years, Peter enjoyed a life of abundance, security and to some extent power and authority. With the death of the Master on the cruel cross of Calvary Peter's hopes and dreams began to fade. With rising persecution and no guaranteed source of income he decided to return to that which he had been called from. What on earth had happened to Christ's promise to Peter with respect to the establishment of His church? The one who was to lead the rest to accomplish God's call and commission, now led them away from it.

Has your dream for a successful ministry begun fading? The LORD will give you direction and counsel. He will lead and direct your life to the place of abundance. You have toiled all night, employed your professional experience, zeal and knowledge, yet nothing seems to move for you. There is nothing indeed which you can show for your labor. At such a time, like the Psalmist, tell yourself *"I lift up my eyes to the hills from where my help comes, my help comes from the LORD the maker of heaven and earth"* (Psalm 121:1-2).

Have you in frustration turned your back to your call? Have you forsaken your vision? The LORD seeks to restore you. Even now He spreads a table before you for you to feast. Will you respond? Will you return? If you will, now is the time.

## Imprisoned Peter

The first two trials in the life of this great apostle of the faith were to bring him to a point where he knew the arm of flesh will fail him, so he would dare not trust his own. This third major trial Peter faced was to prove to him that God's promises are sure to come to pass in spite of opposition from the world.

> *"It was about this time that King Herod arrested some who belonged to the church, intending to persecute them. He had James, the brother of John, put to death with the sword. When he saw that this pleased the Jews; he proceeded to seize Peter also. This happened during the Feast of Unleavened Bread. After arresting him, he put him in prison, handing him over to be guarded by four squads of four soldiers each. Herod intended to bring him out for public trial after the Passover. So Peter was kept in prison, but the church was earnestly praying to God for him. The night before Herod was to bring him to trial, Peter was sleeping between two soldiers, bound with two chains, and sentries stood guard at the entrance. Suddenly an angel of the Lord appeared and a light shone in the cell. He struck Peter on the side and woke him up. 'Quick, get up!' he said, and the chains fell off Peter's wrists. Then the angel said to him, 'Put on your clothes and sandals.' And Peter did so. 'Wrap your cloak around you and follow me,' the angel told him. Peter followed him out of the prison, but he had no idea that what the angel was doing was really happening; he thought he was seeing a vision. They passed the first and second guards and came to the Iron Gate leading to the city. It*

*opened for them by itself, and they went through it. When they had walked the length of one street, suddenly the angel left him. Then Peter came to himself and said, 'Now I know without a doubt that the Lord sent his angel and rescued me from Herod's clutches and from everything the Jewish people were anticipating.' When this had dawned on him, he went to the house of Mary the mother of John, also called Mark, where many people had gathered and were praying. Peter knocked at the outer entrance, and a servant girl named Rhoda came to answer the door. When she recognized Peter's voice, she was so overjoyed she ran back without opening it and exclaimed, 'Peter is at the door!'. 'You're out of your mind,' they told her. When she kept insisting that it was so, they said, 'It must be his angel.' But Peter kept on knocking, and when they opened the door and saw him, they were astonished. Peter motioned with his hand for them to be quiet and described how the Lord had brought him out of prison. 'Tell James and the brothers about this,' he said, and then he left for another place. In the morning, there was no small commotion among the soldiers as to what had become of Peter."* (Acts 12:1-18)

What on earth happened to Christ's promise to Peter?

The one to whom it was said *"whatever you bind on earth would be bound in heaven"* was now bound with two chains. The one to whom it was said *"whatever you loose on earth will be loosed in Heaven"* found himself helplessly bound in chains unable to loose himself. It is but clear that Herod's intent was the public execution of Peter. The intended public trial after the Passover was a mere formality as Peter's fate, like his Master's, was already pre-determined.

I don't know the situation in which you find yourself. You may be bound by life's circumstances, alone in a dark cell unknown by even those who seem to be close to you. Your situation may be so helpless that all you can do is drive yourself to sleep. But I want to let you know there is someone who knows where you are, who sees what is going on, and who hears your every cry. That is no other but your loving and good LORD. The light of God will soon break into that prison. The chains that have held you bound have been broken and soon they will fall off your wrist.

For how long have you slept in despair? God's command to you is *"quick, get up!"* – get up from sleep, get up from where you have fallen. Get up from hopelessness. Herod had his plan for Peter and God had His plan for Peter, according to His eternal plan and purpose. Your enemies may have their plans for you. You may seem to be in their clutches but it is God's plan that will prevail. The LORD of host is about to lead you out of that situation in which you find yourself. The iron gates before you will begin to open by themselves and you will go through unhindered. God is about to break forth into your situation. Will you let Him in?

The good Lord is about to give you an awe-inspiring surprise. I do not know what you have been asking Him but He will soon get you excited by the response He will bring. Above all else be sure of this: God will rather give men in your stead than allow you perish without accomplishing His ordained purpose. The soldiers who guarded Peter were executed in his place.

No matter what Peter went through, in spite of his own failures, God still fulfilled His promise to him. Hallelujah!

# CHAPTER 4

## The Testing of Your Integrity

Many times when God gives a promise, delays come in not just to test our faith but also our integrity. Will you use underhanded methods to bring about what God has promised? Will you take things into your own hands to fulfil God's promises? Have you tried to help God by relying on "other sources" for the fulfilment of your God-ordained destiny?

I will like you to join me as we take a look at the lives of some Bible characters whose integrity God put to the test.

### Abraham

> *"The king of Sodom said to Abram, 'Give me the people and keep the goods for yourself.' But Abram said to the king of Sodom, 'I have raised my hand to the LORD, God Most High, Creator of heaven and earth, and have taken an oath that I will accept nothing belonging to you, not even a thread or the thong of a sandal, so that you will never be able to say, "I made Abram rich." I will accept nothing but what my men have eaten and the share that belongs to the men who went with me – to Aner, Eshcol and Mamre. Let them have their share.'"* (Genesis 14:21-24).

Here we see the patriarch Abraham involved in a rescue operation. He came home with much booty but refused to be rewarded by man. Abraham had a promise from God, this was an *"opportunity"* for him to increase on his wealth and influence at the expense of the king of Sodom but he refused taking advantage of the King and his people who were already in distress hence vulnerable.

What is the level of your integrity? Do you take from others the little they can live on for your personal comfort and luxury? It is very tempting *"when all seems fading"* to resort to underhanded means to get things going, and many do fail this test. Will you refuse the *"secret offers of hope"* from the king of Sodom?

There is an outcry reaching Heaven against men of God who are exploiting their congregation for personal gain and interest. Like Eli God is saying to them *"Why do you scorn my sacrifice and offering that I prescribed for my dwelling? Why do you honor your sons more than me by fattening yourselves on the choice parts of every offering made by my people Israel?"* (1 Samuel 2:29)

And just how many ministers today seem to be fattening their families on the choice part of tithes and offerings made by God's precious people. Too many seem to be anointed; anointed to exploit, and anointed to get the money out of the pockets of those they should be helping.

My dear friend, God will test your integrity and unless you pass this test of financial integrity, before man you may seem very successful but before God you have been disqualified. Resolve in your heart to take advantage of no one for any reason whatsoever. Let God be your only source of blessing. Is it any doubt that after Abraham refused man's reward God revealed Himself to Him as his great reward?

> *"After this, the word of the LORD came to Abram in a vision: "Do not be afraid, Abram. I am your shield, your very great reward"* (Genesis 15:1).

He who looks to man for rewards cannot have God as his reward! God wants to be your reward, even your great reward. Stop looking to man for your needs to be met if God must be your provider. Stop looking to man for help if God must be your helper.

God's greatest problem with Israel was the fact that Israel refused to stand tall and depend on Him only. Time and again Israel went down to Egypt for help. Have we not often turn to the world for help?

> *"Woe to those who go down to Egypt for help, who rely on horses, who trust in the multitude of their chariots and in the great strength of their horsemen, but do not look to the Holy One of Israel, or seek help from the LORD. Yet he too is wise and can bring disaster; he does not take back his words. He will rise up against the house of the wicked, against those who help evildoers. But the Egyptians are men and not God; their horses are flesh and not spirit. When the LORD stretches out his hand, he who helps will stumble, he who is helped will fall; both will perish together"* (Isaiah 31:1-3).

How often has the modern-day Christian turned to this worldly system for help? The LORD says woe to all such. Woe means overwhelming sorrow or heavy affliction and calamity, and this is what God has promised anyone who seeks help apart from Him.

God must be all you go to for help!
God must be all you rely on for help!
God must be all you look up to for help!

When all seems fading, you must pray to God, expect from God, wait on God and receive from a God-ordained channel. God is jealous for all of your attention even *"when all seems fading"*. He wants you to look up to Him–the Holy One of Israel and Him alone. Do not employ worldly methods and counsel and wait on God.

## David

The LORD promised the throne of Israel to the shepherd boy David who came under attack by Saul, the rejected king. Many times David had the opportunity to avenge himself on this one who sought his life and wanted him dead but he refused to take things into his own hands.

Do you take things into your own hands or have allowed vengeance in the hands of God?

It need not be emphasized that Saul made life miserable for David. As time went on, David's dreams faded away. Driven from home, he wandered in the caves, hills and mountains in the desert, and suddenly an opportunity came for him to put an end to Saul's life and consequently to his own pain and suffering (see 1 Samuel 24).

Here David's integrity was at stake, not in the eyes of man but in the eyes of God.

> *"After Saul returned from pursuing the Philistines, he was told, 'David is in the Desert of En Gedi.' So Saul took three thousand chosen men from all Israel and set out to look for David and his men near the Crags of the Wild Goats. He came to the sheep pens along the way; a cave was there, and Saul went in to relieve himself. David and his men were far back in the cave. The men said, 'This is the day the LORD spoke of when he said to you, "I will give your enemy into your hands for you to deal with as you wish."' Then David crept up unnoticed and cut off a corner of Saul's robe. Afterward, David was conscience-stricken for having cut off a corner of his robe. He said to his men, 'The LORD forbid that I should do such a thing to my master, the LORD's anointed, or lift my hand against him; for he is the anointed of the LORD.' With these words David rebuked his men and did not allow them to attack Saul. And Saul left the cave and went his way. Then David went out of the cave and called out to Saul, 'My lord the king!' When Saul looked behind him, David bowed down and prostrated himself with his face to the ground. He said to Saul, 'Why do you listen when men say, "David is bent on harming you"? This day you have seen with your own eyes how the LORD delivered you into my hands in the cave. Some urged me to kill you, but I spared you; I said, "I will not lift my hand against my master, because he is the LORD's anointed." See, my father, look at this piece of your robe in my hand! I cut off the corner of your robe but did not kill*

> you. Now understand and recognize that I am not guilty of wrongdoing or rebellion. I have not wronged you, but you are hunting me down to take my life. May the LORD judge between you and me. And may the LORD avenge the wrongs you have done to me, but my hand will not touch you. As the old saying goes, "From evildoers come evil deeds," so my hand will not touch you. Against whom has the king of Israel come out? Whom are you pursuing? A dead dog? A flea? May the LORD be our judge and decide between us. May he consider my cause and uphold it; may he vindicate me by delivering me from your hand'" (1 Samuel 24:1-15).

Will you allow God to be your judge and avenger? Will you allow Him to uphold your cause? Will you allow him to vindicate you?

David knew the throne was his and even though all seemed to fade away with respect to his ascension to the throne, he refused to use underhanded methods to get there.

Your integrity, my dear friend, will be and must be tested again and again, and resolve in your heart to stand tall.

Some will try in all sincerity to push you to take things into your own hands but like David (see 1 Samuel 26) resolve in your heart to let God have His way and bring about your deliverance in His own time.

# CHAPTER 5

## The testing of The Promise

For a moment I want us to draw some lessons from the life of that great apostle of the Christian church, Paul. In the face of every form of trial and persecution for the sake of the gospel God gave Paul a promise that he would testify about Him in Rome. This promise came when Paul was already in custody and his accusers were pressing for nothing but a death sentence.

> *"The following night the Lord stood near Paul and said, "Take courage! As you have testified about me in Jerusalem, so you must also testify in Rome."* (Acts 23:11)

What are you going through?
What is causing you pain and sorrow?
What is shading your view of the future?

The Word of the LORD to you is *"Take courage"*. Will you open your ears and hear Him speak? Will you receive His Word in your heart? Please do! He says, *"Take courage"*.

This promise of God to Paul in Acts 23:11 was nothing but a confirmation of Paul's vision and purpose - that of spreading the gospel to the gentile lands.

"After all this had happened, Paul decided to go to Jerusalem, passing through Macedonia and Achaia. *"After I have been there,"* he said, *"I must visit Rome also."* (Acts 19:21).

Jerusalem was just meant to be a stop-over in Paul's journey to Rome yet he met a great obstacle; his arrest by the Jews. At such a moment Paul could have thought his prospects to preach this gospel in Rome had ended. He surely became discouraged as he saw all hopes fading. Then the LORD came in to bring hope in a situation where there was little or no hope. From this moment on Paul faced one trial after another before Felix, Festus, Agrippa and Bernice, until the time came for him to sail to Rome under custody.

If there is one thing you should note here, it is that Paul no longer had to worry about his transportation. That was to be taking care of by those who kept him in custody. Though they had in mind that Paul was being taken for trial, through them Paul's vision and God's promise to Paul were being fulfilled. Is it not great that God will use ill intentions of our enemies to fulfil our purpose tied to His promise?

**When favor becomes danger**

Often in desperate moments we tend to accept just any favor offered us. Someone said a drowning man could hold even to a snake if that will cause him to float. A complete reading of Acts 27 and 28 will help you better understand the points we will bring out here. Only the verses of interest will be quoted. Paul and his companions had no easy task sailing from Caesarea to Rome as the forces of nature rose against their journey. With the stormy wind refusing to abate, these guys made a *"forced landing"* in the place called Fair Havens. When much time had been lost, the captain of the ship looked for every opportunity to resume sail.

Paul with the Spirit of discernment warned about the danger that would be involved in such a sail but the people voted for popular opinion and professional counsel instead of listening to the voice of God's prophet;

# The Testing of The Promise

> "But the centurion, instead of listening to what Paul said, followed the advice of the pilot and of the owner of the ship. Since the harbor was unsuitable to winter in, the majority decided that we should sail on, hoping to reach Phoenix and winter there. This was a harbor in Crete, facing both southwest and northwest." (Acts 27: 1-12)

With professional counsel sought and majority vote obtained all was now set for the guys to take off as soon as the least window of opportunity showed up.

> "When a gentle south wind began to blow, they thought they had obtained what they wanted; so they weighed anchor and sailed along the shore of Crete." (Acts 27:13).

"Here it is" they probably said, "We've got to make maximum use of this one before it becomes too late. Forget about this prisoner guy, Paul for a moment". But listen to what happened in the twinkling of an eye: "Before very long, a wind of hurricane force, called the 'northeaster,' swept down from the island. The ship was caught by the storm and could not head into the wind; so we gave way to it and were driven along." (Acts 27: 14-15).

Before we go any further I'll like us to draw out some valuable lessons here

1. Expert advice contrary to divine direction is not worth paying attention to. Never despise the word of a man of God even when it seems to be against professional counsel.
2. Life is not meant for a Christian to live according to majority vote. Hear what God says and stick to it.
3. Not every opportunity is meant for you to dive into; always listen to the voice of the Spirit. Favourable circumstances are not necessarily signs of the divine will.
4. That which appears most often to be favorable turns out not to be.

May be you despised the godly counsel of a man of God and listened to professionals concerning that venture. You saw a *"gentle south wind"* and decided to sail along, and *"before very long a wind of hurricane force, called the northeaster"* has swept against you. Now all seems fading as you are caught in the storm. Your valuables are all gone and you are *"hardly able to make the life boat secure"*. May be you have taken *"such a violent battering from the storm"* that all hopes of coming out safely is gone.

May be for you both the sun and the stars have refused to appear for many days and the storm is continuing its rage against you and you've finally given up all hope of being saved. You look back with regret at the day you dived through that window of opportunity. At such a time acknowledge your error and sin before God and ask Him to intervene.

Let us return to the man in focus, Paul. The Bible says *"when neither sun nor stars appeared for many days and the storm continued raging, we finally gave up all hopes of being saved"* (Acts 27:20). This included Paul, he too like others had given up all hope of seeing his vision and God's promise coming true. The promise of God was under test. Then the Lord decided to step into the scene: *"last night an angel of the God whose I am and whom I serve stood beside me and said, 'do not be afraid, Paul. You must stand trial before Caesar and God has graciously given you the lives of all who sail with you."* (Acts 27:23-24).

When all seems fading see the Lord pointing to you the end. Lift up your eyes above the storm and look to *"Rome"*, where you are heading to.

I do not know where you find yourself at this moment. You intended to travel to "Rome" but now find yourself on a strange island, *"Malta"*, as a result of a shipwreck. Do not fret, God is still in control. He surely has arranged for your stay on that strange shore. Relax and enjoy God's goodness through the Islanders. Let your thoughts about the shipwreck not prevent you from enjoying the *"unusual kindness"* of the Islanders. God has a mission for you in your *"Malta"*, to heal the sick fathers of the Publiuses and to cure the rest of the sick. Let the thoughts of the shipwreck not prevent you from accomplishing God's ordained purpose for you on *"the shore of Malta"*.

When God's set purpose for Paul on Malta was accomplished, God made provisions for him to now sail to Rome. When you cooperate with God on

*The Testing of The Promise*  35

your *"Malta"*, He shall provide an easy head way for you to your *"Rome"*. It might take you three months like Paul, it might take longer than that, it might take shorter than that, do not fear, God is in control. Surely Paul arrived Rome and preached the gospel in fulfilment of his vision tied with God's promise. If we are to give a brief overview of the testing of the promise, we can say in a few lines:

God gave Paul a promise to testify about Him in Rome and nothing could stop that.

1. There were trials (Felix's, Festus', Agrippa's)
2. There were plots to kill him (Acts 23)
3. There was a shipwreck (Acts 27)
4. There was an attempted execution (27:42)
5. There was a viper attack (28:3).

But none of these could annul the promise.

# CHAPTER 6

## When You Fell Like Giving Up

---

When all seems fading, one can continue to press on with hopes that things will soon change for the better. However, it becomes a totally different situation when instead of a determination to press on there comes a resignation. Even in such a situation, God longs to reach out and bring hope to what, in our blurred vision, may appear hopeless.

Let us take a look at the lives of the heroes of the faith and see what valuable lessons, we as individuals may draw from there.

### Elijah at the end of the road

*"Now Ahab told Jezebel everything Elijah had done and how he had killed all the prophets with the sword. So Jezebel sent a messenger to Elijah to say, "May the gods deal with me, be it ever so severely, if by this time tomorrow I do not make your life like that of one of them." Elijah was afraid and ran for his life. When he came to Beersheba in Judah, he left his servant there, while he himself went a day's journey into the desert. He came to a broom tree, sat down under it and prayed that he might die. "I have had enough, LORD," he said. "Take my life; I am no better than my ancestors." Then he lay down under the tree and fell asleep. All at once an angel touched him and said, "Get up and eat." He looked around, and there by his head was*

*a cake of bread baked over hot coals, and a jar of water. He ate and drank and then lay down again. The angel of the LORD came back a second time and touched him and said, "Get up and eat, for the journey is too much for you." So he got up and ate and drank. Strengthened by that food, he travelled forty days and forty nights until he reached Horeb, the mountain of God."* (1 Kings 19:1- 8)

No one is superhuman. There are moments when even mighty men like Elijah feel like giving it up. This was a prophet to whom God had revealed himself in diverse ways; through miracles of provision by ravens and through a widow (see 1 Kings 17); through the demonstration of God's power by calling down fire from Heaven to consume the sacrifice (see 1 Kings 18).

Elijah had established his authority as the prophet of the LORD before the King by ordering the execution of the prophets of Baal; Elijah shut the heavens for three and a half years so that there was no rain. Can you imagine this same mighty man of God running from the threat of Jezebel? Surely God allowed this to happen so Elijah could depend more on Him.

The Bible says *"Elijah was afraid..."*
- What is it that is causing you fear?
- What makes you afraid when you are all alone?
- What brings you a sense of insecurity even in the midst of people?
- For how long have you been running and hiding?
- What seems to be hunting your life?
- Is that same thing driving you away from home into the wilderness of defeat and failure?
- Have you felt like giving up lately?

*"He came to a broom tree, sat down under it and prayed that he might die"*

Have you desired death to life? Life's worries and difficulties and troubles have overwhelmed you and you see no reason, absolutely none, to pray for strength to endure. You now find it easier to pray for death.

*"I have had enough, LORD"*
Do you tell yourself it is more than you can bear? You seem to tell God *"my cup is full I can't take this anymore"*

For how long have you sat under that tree of despair? You seem to have no desire to move on.

Commenting on this passage, Chuck Swindoll says, *"The most damaging impact of self-pity is its ultimate end. Cuddle and nurse it as an infant, and you'll have on your hands in a brief period of time a beast, a monster, a raging, coarse brute that will spread the poison of bitterness and paranoia throughout your system. You will soon discover that the sea of self-pity has brought with it prickly urchins of doubt, despair, and even the desire to die".* (Living insights study Bible page 358, Zondervan).

Even under that tree of hopelessness and despair God wants to reach out to you. He is preparing a table for you from where you can derive strength to move on.

Do you see that most often we do not really know what we need? Not even how much we need? Elijah thought he needed to die but God saw that all he needed was something to bring back his strength. May you and I be sensitive to God's angels assigned to provide us what we need! Elijah ate and thought that was enough. But God knew it wasn't enough and got him up the second time to eat and drink, knowing all that was ahead.

What lessons do we draw from here?

1. Never give self-pity a foothold, for it soon takes over your whole person.
2. God is more concerned about that situation of yours than you think.
3. One may think he is prepared enough but only God knows how much you need to face the task ahead of you.
4. When you feel like giving up, the best place for you is not under a broom tree but at Horeb, the mountain of God. Run to the shelter

of the Most High and find refuge there. Pour out your heart before his throne and receive ministry from your Counsellor, your Comforter and Guide.

## Moses at the edge of the cliff

When someone is at the edge of the cliff, what comes to your mind is suicide or murder. At such a time in Moses' life all that this mighty servant of God could think of was death. Is there any doubt that those without Christ when faced with despair resort to suicide? There is need to bless the LORD daily for the hope you have in Him.

> *"Moses heard the people of every family wailing, each at the entrance to his tent. The LORD became exceedingly angry, and Moses was troubled. He asked the LORD, "Why have you brought this trouble on your servant? What have I done to displease you that you put the burden of all these people on me? Did I conceive all these people? Did I give them birth? Why do you tell me to carry them in my arms, as a nurse carries an infant, to the land you promised on oath to their forefathers? Where can I get meat for all these people? They keep wailing to me, 'Give us meat to eat!' I cannot carry all these people by myself; the burden is too heavy for me. If this is how you are going to treat me, put me to death right now--if I have found favor in your eyes--and do not let me face my own ruin."* (Number 11:10 - 15)

We see this mighty prophet whom God has used so mightily to bring the Israelites out of Egypt. Through Moses God performed outstanding miracles, divided the red sea, brought about outstanding victories over the enemies of Israel. How on earth could Moses arrive in this *"state of despondency"*? Is that which the Lord has called you to do such a burden? Seek the face of God and He will lead you on what to do for the burden to become light. Maybe you have been struggling to do it all by yourself.

The danger of despondency is that it causes even the mighty to doubt the power of the Almighty God. When God promised to provide what the people craved for, who could tell that even Moses would doubt God?

*When You Fell Like Giving Up* 41

> "But Moses said, "Here I am among six hundred thousand men on foot, and you say, 'I will give them meat to eat for a whole month!' Would they have enough if flocks and herds were slaughtered for them? Would they have enough if all the fish in the sea were caught for them?" The LORD answered Moses, "Is the LORD's arm too short? You will now see whether or not what I say will come true for you." (Number 11: 21- 22).

The Lord promised abundance of meat. All Moses needed was to believe the Lord whom he had walked with all this while.

There's a great lesson to draw from here:
No matter the extent to which you have been used by God, no matter your anointing, no matter your "security" once you take your eyes off God and focus on your environment and raging circumstances, things just begin to go down the drain and the only solution is to lift up your eyes to the One whose arm is not too short. This is all God asked Moses, to remind him of the God he was dealing with:

> "Is the Lord's arm too short? You will now see whether or not what I say will come true for you."

Again, may I say that, what God has promised you will surely come true. You can trust Him.

## David without strength to weep

> "David and his men reached Ziklag on the third day. Now the Amalekites had raided the Negev and Ziklag. They had attacked Ziklag and burned it, and had taken captive the women and all who were in it, both young and old. They killed none of them, but carried them off as they went on their way. When David and his men came to Ziklag, they found it destroyed by fire and their wives and sons and daughters taken captive. So David and his men wept aloud until they had no strength left to weep. David's two wives had been captured--Ahinoam of Jezreel and Abigail, the widow of Nabal of

> *Carmel. David was greatly distressed because the men were talking of stoning him; each one was bitter in spirit because of his sons and daughters. But David found strength in the LORD his God."* (1 Samuel 30:1- 6)

At this time, Saul who sought David's life had driven him from his homeland. He had succeeded to settle at Ziklag after years of wondering from one mountain, hill or cave to another. Then a disaster struck and everyone turned against David. Even his own men who had pledged their loyalty to him now turned against him and talked of stoning him.

Is all that you worked for seem gone in the split of a second? For David it was his two wives but for you it can be all your finances. It can be your home crumbling; the company you formed may be crumbling. The very people you have trained are now turning against you. You are blamed for all their misfortunes and losses.

The Bible says, *"So David and his men wept allowed until they had no strength left to weep."*

Even the warriors, mighty men of valor, have their time of weeping. There are some who think weeping is a sign of weakness but it isn't. There are moments when the best to do is to weep. There are moments when others will help you find strength in God, and all of us need at least someone in our lives who in times of sorrow and discouragement will help us find strength in God. David had one such in his life, Jonathan.

In the face of suffering and wandering the Bible says, *"While David was at Horesh in the Desert of Ziph, he learned that Saul had come to take his life. And Saul's son Jonathan went to David at Horesh and helped him to find strength in God."* (1 Samuel 23:15-16). However, times come when there is no one to encourage us, all that comes from without is opposition and discouraging attitudes and statements. It is exactly in such a condition which David found himself. But instead of losing hope the Bible says, *"but David encouraged himself in the LORD his God."* (1 Samuel 30: 6b KJV).

My dear friend, there are times you should and must encourage yourself to move on. When everyone else has turned against you, encourage yourself in the Lord your God and move on.

As He did to David, if only you encourage yourself to move on, God will restore to you what the enemy has stolen from you. He is more than able to do it. Praise His holy name!

> *"David recovered everything the Amalekites had taken, including his two wives. Nothing was missing: young or old, boy or girl, plunder or anything else they had taken. David brought everything back. He took all the flocks and herds, and his men drove them ahead of the other livestock, saying, "This is David's plunder."* (1 Samuel 30:18 - 20)

# CHAPTER 7

## When You Have Given Up

---

*"Early the next morning Abraham took some food and a skin of water and gave them to Hagar. He set them on her shoulders and then sent her off with the boy. She went on her way and wandered in the desert of Beersheba. When the water in the skin was gone, she put the boy under one of the bushes. Then she went off and sat down nearby, about a bowshot away, for she thought, "I cannot watch the boy die." And as she sat there nearby, she began to sob. God heard the boy crying, and the angel of God called to Hagar from heaven and said to her, "What is the matter, Hagar? Do not be afraid; God has heard the boy crying as he lies there. Lift the boy up and take him by the hand, for I will make him into a great nation." Then God opened her eyes and she saw a well of water. So she went and filled the skin with water and gave the boy a drink. God was with the boy as he grew up. He lived in the desert and became an archer. (Genesis 21:14-20).*

Before this episode in Hagar's life, things had begun fading and she already attempted to give up. Hagar was a housemaid whom her mistress considered an avenue to build a family line for herself. (See Genesis 16:1-9).

When Hagar had gained enough ground and found enough favor before Abraham she thought she had gotten what she wanted. She had nursed sacred ambitions of becoming the new mistress. *"When she knew she was preg-*

*nant, she began to despise her mistress."* Ambition becomes a great disease if not properly handled.

Many people, like Hagar, find themselves today in a state of hopelessness as a result of their pride and arrogance. Others are like Sarah. Sarah was interested in nothing but herself. Selfishness is the root cause of all disobedience and instability in every environment. It was her family line she wanted to build. Now self-pity will not allow her build this family line and she tends to blame everybody around. She wanted to manipulate everybody for her personal gain.

Are you a manipulator? Your manipulation will catch up with you. Only death to self-pity can set you free from all tendencies to manipulate. The manipulator likes to do whatever is best in his or her own eyes forgetting that doing whatever seems best to her will mean:
- Trampling on the opinions of others
- Hurting others.

The manipulator wants to be in absolute control directly or indirectly and is always concerned only about her own interest. Sarah who wanted no "emotional torture" from Hagar now maltreated Hagar.

Manipulators do to others what they do not want others to do to them.

Manipulators blame everybody for the bad things happening in their lives.

Are you caught in the web of your manipulations? Bitterness and retaliation is not and can never be the solution. At this time in Hagar's life her ambitions of becoming Abraham's new mistress started to fade as *"Sarah ill-treated Hagar"* and the only way out for her, so she thought, was to flee.

When all seems fading around you, the best thing to do is

1. To confront the cause of the crises and not to escape. Escape can only make you a fugitive and never a freed man.

2. Find a solution to the crisis. This always consists of doing the right thing. The solution to every problem lies in doing the right thing from the believer's point of view.

Here the cause of the crisis in Hagar's life was her arrogant attitude to authority, and all she was supposed to do was submit to her mistress and not try to escape. God's recommendation to Hagar was to go back and submit to her mistress.

Has your ambition or arrogance landed you in trouble? Submission is the solution. There's no solution in escaping from reality but in confronting it. There are many ways to run from a problem:

1. Ignoring the problem.
2. Acknowledging the problem but pretending to have had a solution to it.
3. Literally running away.

None of the above can bring a lasting solution. The only way out is to seek a solution.

Hagar had had a promise from the LORD (see Genesis 16:10-12) and she lived in total anticipation of what this boy Ishmael will become. She had hoped that he would be the heir to Abraham, after all even if Sarah conceived, Ishmael remained the first child. Her crisis reached its apex when Abraham sent her and her son packing with just some food and a jar of water. It is clear that Hagar was sent away from home because of Ishmael and thus her whole life was now tied to that of this boy. Without a father, without a mother, alone with a son whom because of circumstances was now rejected by the father, without a home, without shelter, with nowhere to call her home Hagar wandered in the desert. Without the direction of a mistress or a master or her dream husband Hagar wandered aimlessly in the desert, not knowing where to go.

Have you been driven from home?

May be you just find yourself away from home and there's no one you can run to for help or support. May be in your life there is no longer anyone to give you counsel and direction, you feel abandoned. May be you are a single mom struggling all alone with kids whose irresponsible father has refused to cater for. It's time to turn to your Father in Heaven and hand everything to Him.

All what Hagar had to sustain her and the boy was now exhausted and they were left with nothing in the site. That which fuelled your vision is now exhausted and there's nowhere else to go for a refill and you wander what becomes of it. Hagar's only hope for the future was in Ishmael and now in her frustration she laid him in a bush waiting for the boy to die.

Have you out of frustration abandoned your dream and vision? All around you has faded and circumstances have pushed you to abandon your vision. The vision you once held tight in your arms now lies under the brush of the bushes in the desert of your wandering.

Hagar said, *"I can't watch the body die"*. Will you bear to watch that vision perish? Have you moved a bowshot away separating yourself from your dying vision? God has heard your cry and has seen those tears you shed.

Hagar could only sob, may be because she was now too weary to cry out loud. For you the tears may just be flowing within, you have cried time and again inwardly but appeared strong on the outside. God has seen even those tears of the heart.

*"God heard the boy crying"*; it is not only your cries that God hears, but that of your abandoned vision is reaching up to Him. The cries of your perishing hope have ascended to the throne of the King and He will never remain indifferent.

> *"Lift up the boy and take him by the hand, for I will make him in to a great nation."*

My friend it's time to hope again. It's time to pick up the vision you've abandoned and take it by hand out of the bush of despair. As you pick it up God will open your eyes to wells of ideas and favor. He is about opening your eyes to a source of abundance. That which has been there always which you or others couldn't see before, God is about opening your eyes to see, yes to see a well that won't run dry, which no one can stop, from which you can always refill. It is time to hope again and start refuelling your vision. Start nurturing it again.

God wants to help you accomplish and fulfil that vision.

The place that was meant to be burial ground for your vision shall become the place of its rebirth. As *"God was with the boy as he grew up"* so will He stand with your vision as it grows to maturity even though no one else stands with you.

# CHAPTER 8

## The Power of Obedience

---

Acts of obedience -when all seems to fade in one's life - are tremendous avenues for the release of power to carry you along. In this chapter, I'll like us to draw lessons from two people: Noah and Abraham.

**Noah**

The secret of Noah's walk with God lay in the fact that:

1. He did all that God commanded him to do (Genesis 7:5)
2. He did everything just as God commanded him (Genesis 6:22).

Noah was in the face of mockery and spite as he stepped out in faith to build the first ship on dry ground, far from the closest shore. But in faith he held on to doing what God asked him to do, adding nothing and subtracting nothing. The only reason why Noah and all his family were saved is because Noah did all just as he was asked to do, he neither added to God's design of the ark nor made the least modifications.

How many are sinking today in the floodwaters of life just because they decided to add or modify God's dimensions of the ark, which was meant to save them? How many are drowned today because in the face of a condemned, mocking world, they stopped building the ark that was meant to keep them afloat?

You have got to hold unto that which God is asking you to do, that will be your lifeboat in the face of calamity. Endure the laughter, endure the mockery, appear foolish to everyone else but the God who asked you to do it.

> *"For forty days the flood kept coming on the earth, and as the waters increased they lifted the ark high above the earth. The waters rose and increased greatly on the earth, and the ark floated on the surface of the water. They rose greatly on the earth, and all the high mountains under the entire heavens were covered. The waters rose and covered the mountains to a depth of more than twenty feet."* (Genesis 7:17-20)

God's will for Noah at this time was for him to be in the ark. When a man is where God wants him to be, when God wants him to be there, doing what God wants him to do, problems, storms and difficulties cannot destroy him. Though he may find himself in the same situation of trials and difficulties and storms with others, the same storms or flood waters which will cause others to sink and drown will only help lift him up high above the natural, high above his peers. Floodwaters come to lift you up; they come to take you to heights you will otherwise not reach.

Without the flood waters, the highest point Noah could ever have reached is the peak of the highest mountain, but the floodwaters took him to six meters higher than the highest mountain. These floodwaters could only be favorable to Noah while others were drowning because he had obeyed God in everything as he was commanded.

Will it be too much to say the floodwaters took Noah's ark for a pleasure ride? Like Noah, your storms of life will lift you up and take you for spiritual, emotional, and financial pleasure rides when others are sinking, if you resolve to do everything, as God commands you.

Just as the floodwaters in Noah's days did not recede until Noah had been lifted to the highest point, the floodwaters of your life will not recede until they have lifted you to your God-ordained heights. Only God can cause the floodwaters to recede but until they have accomplished the purpose for which He allowed them He will not cause them to recede.

**Are your floodwaters lasting longer than you expected?**

God gave Noah a command to get into the ark and when he had done so, the Bible says, *"Then the LORD shut him in"*.

Noah became impatient in the ark; he couldn't wait for God to tell him to come out but kept on sending out doves and ravens in order to know how far the waters had receded.

Like Noah impatience will lead you to unnecessary and useless adventures and ventures, trying to find out the level of your floodwaters. For how long have you been trying things out instead of just staying where God had placed you? For how long will you continue to be impatient with God's workings in your life and environment?

Wait in your ark upon the flood waters till God asks you to come out (Genesis 8:15). Do not try to know how much longer it will take for your floodwaters to recede completely. Trust in the One who shut you in to bring you out when appropriate.

**Abraham**

No other person in scripture benefited from the power of prompt obedience to the voice of God like Abraham did.

There is power in instant obedience to the voice of the Holy Spirit. There is tremendous power in acting fast on that which God reveals. I would want us to examine some instances where Abraham manifested prompt obedience.

1. "***On that very day*** *Abraham took his son Ishmael and all those born in his household or bought with his money, every male in his household, and circumcised them, as God told him*" (Genesis 17: 23, emphasis mine).

   Here God entered the covenant of circumcision with Abraham; he decided to enter into the experience immediately.

   There is no blessing in procrastination. It renders a man powerless and ineffective. Abraham never feared the pains and risk that were involved in having everybody in his household circumcised on the same day. This could render them powerless and unable to defend themselves in the face of any attack.

2. "*The matter distressed Abraham greatly because it concerned his son. But God said to him, 'Do not be so distressed about the boy and your maidservant. Listen to whatever Sarah tells you, because it is through Isaac that your offspring will be reckoned. I will make the son of the maidservant into a nation also, because he is your offspring.'* ***Early the next morning*** *Abraham took some food and a skin of water and gave them to Hagar. He set them on her shoulders and then sent her off with the boy. She went on her way and wandered in the desert of Beersheba*" (Genesis 21:11 – 14, emphasis mine).

   Emphasis is on the phrase *"Early the next morning..."* This was not an easy thing to do. The Bible says, *"The matter distressed Abraham greatly"*, it is not as though he had been looking for an opportunity to send away Hagar and Ishmael but he certainly knew obedience was the only way out. Once God had spoken there was no need to bargain. Abraham was sending away the first symbol of his strength and only someone committed to obedience could act with such promptness.

   Never give yourself enough time to raise questions and doubts about what God says. Do not give yourself enough time to raise objections.

3. "*Sometime later God tested Abraham. He said to him, 'Abraham!' 'Here I am,' he replied. Then God said, 'Take your son, your only son, Isaac, whom you love, and go to the region of Moriah. Sacrifice him*

> *there as a burnt offering on one of the mountains I will tell you about.' Early the next morning Abraham got up and saddled his donkey. He took with him two of his servants and his son Isaac. When he had cut enough wood for the burnt offering, he set out for the place God had told him about. On the third day Abraham looked up and saw the place in the distance. He said to his servants, 'Stay here with the donkey while I and the boy go over there. We will worship and then we will come back to you.'"* (Genesis 22:1–5, emphasis, mine)

It wasn't very long since Abraham sent away his son Ishmael at the request of God. Before he recovered from that incident, another command came, this time around to sacrifice his remaining son Isaac as a burnt offering. One can say, with Ishmael there was still hope that his father could one day meet again with him but not so with Isaac. God demanded the life of Isaac and one could have thought Abraham would think it over and over but *"early the next morning..."*. This is a man who had discovered the power of prompt obedience and not even the pain and loss involved could cause him to delay his obedience. He had discovered that delayed obedience is disobedience. "Here I am" is a statement that goes beyond an ordinary response to a call. It's a statement that expresses readiness, commitment and availability.

Isaac represented all Abraham now had. He was the evidence of God's miracle in his life. The one for whom Abraham had worked so hard. By asking for Isaac God was asking for all that Abraham had. Moreover, God ensured that Abraham did not act out of emotions, so he had to take at least a three day journey to the place of his sacrifice. To have walked for three days without any attempt to turn back expresses a total, complete and wholehearted commitment to a life of obedience. Until you have been tested and approved and continuously tested and approved, do not expect to be used by God.

After three days Abraham still saw the place of his sacrifice from a distance. You should not expect to arrive at the place of brokenness so soon. You cannot reach there in a day and you cannot hasten it. To reach that place you must carry your all, make up your mind to get there and tread the road with faith and surrendering. When all seems fading, know that there is power in obedience even when it comes with pain and suffering. Obedience will cause you to soar on wings like eagles. Allow God to lead you to the place of brokenness.

## Crossing your Jabbok

There's a point in each person's walk with God where he must be separated from all he dreams of and has worked for to own. For Hagar it was Beersheba, for Abraham it was mount Moriah, for Jacob it was Jabbok.

> *"That night Jacob got up and took his two wives, his two maidservants and his eleven sons and crossed the ford of the Jabbok. After he had sent them across the stream, he sent over all his possessions. So Jacob was left alone, and a man wrestled with him till daybreak. When the man saw that he could not overpower him, he touched the socket of Jacob's hip so that his hip was wrenched as he wrestled with the man. Then the man said, 'Let me go, for it is daybreak.' But Jacob replied, "I will not let you go unless you bless me." The man asked him, 'What is your name?' 'Jacob,' he answered. Then the man said, 'Your name will no longer be Jacob, but Israel, because you have struggled with God and with men and have overcome.' Jacob said, 'Please tell me your name.' But he replied, 'Why do you ask my name?' Then he blessed him there. So Jacob called the place Peniel, saying, 'It is because I saw God face to face, and yet my life was spared.' The sun rose above him as he passed Peniel, and he was limping because of his hip."* (Genesis 32: 22-31).

There must come a time when you are separated from all that you possess. In this pilgrim journey there must be a Jabbok Ford for you. At Jabbok you are separated from all your possessions, delights, and company so that you can be left alone for God to deal with. Note that Jacob separated himself from all his possessions and sent them in the direction of the promise land. As a result, there was no possibility of turning back to Aram since all his possessions were on God's side, for *"where your treasure is there your heart is"*.

God will ensure that your heart is in Heaven before He brings about your final breaking. Many of us are still unbroken because our treasures and therefore our hearts are still here on this judged world. At times, the question you should ask yourself when things just seem fading is:

*"What is that desire or treasures I must let go, that sacrifice I must make so that I can be left alone for God to deal with me?"* He needs your total surrender and thus will continue to wrestle with you until you reach the point of total dependence upon Him. He is committed to break your self-strength so that in you there can be a true God-hunger. He wants to ruin the self in you so you can start living the fullness of God.

# CHAPTER 9

## The Power of Surrending

Just as power is released to carry the obedient person along, enormous spiritual power is released for the surrendered individual. The last chapter ended with the need for a Jabbok - the place of separation and breaking. At Jabbok God destroys and dislocates that which prevents your total dependence on Him and causes you to depend wholly, totally and completely on Him. It is at this point that He changes the face of your interactions with Him. He wants you to reach the point where you will see Him face to face and your life will be spared.

After Jabbok the next place in your walk with God is Peniel. Jabbok means *"flowing"*. As you allow God's will to *"flow"* through you, as you allow His breaking to flow through you, then can you reach Peniel. Peniel means *"face of God"*. In the wrestling Jacob saw the face of God. A man who sought the hand of God throughout this life now came in contact with not just the hand of God but also the face of God. You know, when Jacob was fleeing to Aram, all what he could ask was for God's blessings, the hand of God. This same hand that blessed him now had to carry out a painful dislocation thus revealing His face to Jacob.

When Jacob was fleeing from Esau, the Bible says, *"When he reached a certain place, he stopped for the night because the sun had set. Taking one of the stones there, he put it under his head and lay down to sleep."*

- Has the sun set for you?
- Do you feel that the night has been so long?
- Is your headrest a stone?

Even right there God is with you, He longs to take you to Jabbok. After Jabbok, things become different. The Bible says, *"The sun rose above him as he passed Peniel"* (Genesis 32: 30). This means all the time Jacob was in Paddan Aram, it was really night for him. No doubt all the painful toil and labor and sweating. Twenty years plus, what a long night that was!

Why is God so desperate for you to reach Jabbok? Not because He delights in breaking His children but because He delights in what they become after they have been broken. He wants you to come to this point so that the sun will rise above you as you pass Peniel. As you pass Peniel what comes after is brightness, splendor, humility and gentleness. After Peniel the face of man becomes like the face of God. You will begin to honor those whom God has exalted above you; you plead with them to accept your gift. Who could imagine Jacob the grabber now bowing down to man? Jabbok destroys greed, selfishness, self-justification and self-protection. At Jabbok, Jacob's whole future was changed; he was given a new name, thus separated from his past.

From Jabbok onward, Jacob honored God as *"El Elohe Israel"* - *"mighty is the God of Israel"*. He was no longer just *"The God of my father, the God of Abraham and the Fear of Isaac"* but He was now a personal God, a mighty one for that matter. God wants to become personal to you; as a God mighty in power, in provision, in holiness, in humility, in protection.

Will you be bold enough to ask God to take you to Jabbok? Because after every Jabbok, *"the sun of righteousness will rise with healing in its wings. And you will go out and leap like calves released from the stall."* (Malachi 4:2)

It did not just happen to Jacob, it happened to the apostles of old.

> "You do not want to leave to, do you?" Jesus asked the twelve. Simon Peter answered him, "Lord, to whom else shall we go? You have the words of eternal life." (John 6: 67-69).

Jabbok is the point of no return, where the Savior truly becomes Lord of your life. It is the point of total surrendering of your own dreams and will to His, it is the point of finding yourself totally helpless and useless without the Savior, the point where you can sincerely ask:

"Lord, to whom shall I go?"
"Lord, on what else shall I rely?"
"Lord, how shall I live?"
"Lord, where shall I go?"

And find the answers in Him alone.

One of the great benefits of surrendering is fulfilment. You cannot know any true satisfaction or fulfilment until you have surrendered. Jabbok is not only a point of breaking and surrendering, but also of total abandonment. It is a point of "no return", a point where all bridges behind you have been broken for each forward step taken; a point where there is absolutely nowhere and no one else to run to. This is the point where Christianity becomes heaven on earth.

## The most Powerful Prayer

The most powerful prayer is one that expresses surrendering. No one can fight for too long with God's will. It is no problem to come in disagreement with God's will but every servant of God at such moments must say, *"Not my will but yours be done"*. That is the most powerful prayer any human can ever make, for it moves no other mountain but the mountain of self.

> "Lord, I do not see it the way you say, however not my will but yours be done".

When the angel Gabriel revealed to Mary God's will, her final words in that conversation were *"I am the Lord's servant, may it be to me as you have said"* (Luke 1:38).

As a servant of God He alone knows what He wants to make of you. He plans to make you an instrument in His hands, even a threshing-sledge (See Isaiah 41:15-16):

- New
- Sharp
- With many teeth.

This takes yielding and total surrendering. God must take you into His workshop for you to undergo painful bending, painful cutting, painful breaking, painful hammering and painful filing so that you be a very useful instrument in His hands. So when all seems fading thank Him for all that He is doing in your life.

Daily you must the tell LORD *"May it be as you have planned and purposed. I am willing to be used by you wherever, whenever, however, in whatever capacity"*. That's what the statement *"I am the Lord's servant…"* means. Faith exercises its power greatest in surrendering. Remember when Peter said *"But because you say so…"* (Luke 5: 5b) and actually obeyed the Lord, it brought about the greatest experience Peter ever had in his fishing career. It might not match with physical evidences but because He says so…

In that prayer lies your strength, do not be afraid to pray it as often as you have breath.

# CHAPTER 10

## The Power of Tears

Many people have the impression, a wrong one of course, that tears are an expression of weakness. They think the strong do not cry even when it pains, all the strong can do is cry within them and prove strong on the outside. I want to let you know that there is power in tears; not tears of deceit or self-pity but genuine tears, which flow when a man desperately cries for help. The Israelites knew this: they had to cry out to God whenever they found themselves in oppression. When some people manage to cry, they are often cries of self-pity, cries of regret, cries of pain rather than cries for help. Isaiah said *"O people of Zion, who live in Jerusalem, you will weep no more. How gracious He will be when you cry for help! As soon as He hears, He will answer you."* (Isaiah 30:19, italics, mine).

Many times when people cry, they cry about the pain and wish help could come but never cry out for help. Crying usually shows how desperate a man is and how urgent help is needed. The Bible says, *"as soon as He hears"*. How will He hear if you do not cry out for help? There is power in your crying for help, the Bible says, *"God longs to be gracious"* and He will surely respond, not to your cry of self-pity, but to your cry for help. Just read the following verses

> *"During that long period, the king of Egypt died. The Israelites groaned in their slavery and cried out, and their cry for help because of their slavery*

went up to God. God heard their groaning and he remembered his covenant with Abraham, with Isaac and with Jacob. So God looked on the Israelites and was concerned about them." (Exodus 2:23-25)

"The LORD said, "I have indeed seen the misery of my people in Egypt. I have heard them crying out because of their slave drivers, and I am concerned about their suffering. So I have come down to rescue them from the hand of the Egyptians and to bring them up out of that land into a good and spacious land, a land flowing with milk and honey--the home of the Canaanites, Hittites, Amorites, Perizzites, Hivites and Jebusites." (Exodus 3:7-8)

"Our forefathers went down into Egypt, and we lived there many years. The Egyptians mistreated us and our fathers, 16 but when we cried out to the LORD, he heard our cry and sent an angel and brought us out of Egypt." (Numbers 20:15-16a)

"But they cried to the LORD for help, and he put darkness between you and the Egyptians; he brought the sea over them and covered them. You saw with your own eyes what I did to the Egyptians. Then you lived in the desert for a long time." (Joshua 24:7)

"In my distress I called to the LORD; I cried to my God for help. From his temple he heard my voice; my cry came before him, into his ears." (Psalm 18:6).

Have you been crying to yourself or to God? Have your tears been those of self-pity and regret rather than of the need for help? Do you consider tears as a sign of weakness? Are you in pain? Does all seem fading? Do you see as though all hope is gone? Then my advice for you is the same the prophet Jeremiah gave to his people, "The hearts of the people cry out to the Lord. O wall of the Daughter of Zion let your tears flow like a river day and night; give yourself no relief, your eyes no rest. Arise, cry out in the night, as the watches of the night begin; pour out your heart like water in the presence of the Lord. Lift up your hands to him for the lives of your children, who faint from hunger at the head of every street." (Lamentations 2:18-19).

Of the Lord Jesus it is said, *"During the days of Jesus' life on earth, he offered up prayers with loud cries and tears to the one who could save him from death, and he was heard because of his reverend submission."* (Hebrews 5:7). Now is that weakness? Is that failure? Certainly not! Change your mentality and learn to cry out for help, let the tears flow when they have to, do not hold them back. Crying is a means of releasing anger, hurt, resentment, and bitterness if it is sincere and directed to God. Crying brings freedom to the soul and causes relief as it brings down God's intervention.

- Are you sick? Cry out for healing!
- Are you in bondage? Cry out for deliverance!
- Are you oppressed? Cry out for salvation!
- Are you distressed? Cry out for comfort!
- Are you in need? Cry out for provision!

There's no need to pretend that all is Okay. There's no need trying to hold back the tears, let them flow out, after all God responds to persistent cries and tears!

> *"And will not God bring about justice for his chosen ones, who cry out to him day and night? Will he keep putting them off? I tell you, he will see that they get justice, and quickly."* (Luke 18:7-8a).

# CHAPTER 11

## The Power of the Altar

---

Every altar in the Bible was erected for one or more of three reasons, I believe. These three reasons give me my definition for the three kinds of altars, which I have discovered.

1. **An altar of prayer:**

   *"From there he went on toward the hills east of Bethel and pitched his tent, with Bethel on the west and Ai on the east. There he built an altar to the LORD and called on the name of the LORD."(Genesis 12:8)*

   *"Isaac built an altar there and called on the name of the LORD. There he pitched his tent, and there his servants dug a well."(Genesis 26:25)*

There's no mention of sacrifice here on any of these altars. Not on the altar by Abraham or that by Isaac. We are just told they built an altar and called on the name of the LORD. This calling on the name of the Lord is nothing but prayer. Prayer is some kind of an altar. When you pray, you are raising up an altar to God.

2. **An altar of sacrifice.**

   *"Then Noah built an altar to the LORD and, taking some of all the clean animals and clean birds, he sacrificed burnt offerings on it."* (Genesis 8:20)

   *"When they reached the place God had told him about, Abraham built an altar there and arranged the wood on it. He bound his son Isaac and laid him on the altar, on top of the wood."* (Genesis 22:9)

These altars were built for the expressed purpose of sacrificing to God, for the offering of personal sacrifices by those who built them. Each time we carry out an act of sacrifice, may be to the need of someone, or give sacrificially to God beyond your usual giving, you raise up an altar of sacrifice to God.

3. **Altar of praise and worship.**

   *"There he set up an altar and called it El Elohe Israel."* (Genesis 33:20)

   *"The LORD appeared to Abram and said, "To your offspring I will give this land." So he built an altar there to the LORD, who had appeared to him".* (Genesis 12:7)

Jacob did not offer any sacrifice on this altar; neither did he call on the name of the Lord. All he did was to call the altar *"El Elohe Israel" - "Mighty is the God of Israel"*. Hence this was an altar of worship and praise. The purpose of the altar was to magnify the name of His God. When we praise and worship God, especially in difficult moments we are actually raising up altars to Him.

Each one of us must learn to build altars; not physical structures but spiritual monuments in your walk with God. Most of us have experienced the power of the altar of prayer only; others have experienced also the power of the altar of praise and worship but few have realized the tremendous power that could be released in your favor if only an altar of sacrifice were raised. There is a call for believers to begin raising altars of sacrifices in their lives to orchestrate breakthroughs that will otherwise not come.

*The Power of the Altar*

When Noah raised an altar of sacrifice in Gen 8: 20, the Bible says

> *"The LORD smelled the pleasing aroma and said in his heart: "Never again will I curse the ground because of man, even though every inclination of his heart is evil from childhood. And never again will I destroy all living creatures, as I have done. As long as the earth endures, seedtime and harvest, cold and heat, summer and winter, day and night will never cease."*
> (Genesis 8:21- 22)

> *"Then God blessed Noah and his sons, saying to them, "Be fruitful and increase in number and fill the earth. The fear and dread of you will fall upon all the beasts of the earth and all the birds of the air, upon every creature that moves along the ground, and upon all the fish of the sea; they are given into your hands. Everything that lives and moves will be food for you. Just as I gave you the green plants, I now give you everything."* (Genesis 9:1- 3)

Do you see what happened? Noah's sacrifice provoked God to make far-reaching proclamations and blessings over Noah and his children. Dear friend, where the altar of prayer has not worked, where the altar of worship has not worked either, the altar of sacrifice will. It did for Noah! It did for Abraham too. When Abraham built an altar to sacrifice his only son, he was laying down his all on the altar of sacrifice and the response from God was awesome. (See Genesis 22: 11-18).

God can be a debtor to no one; you cannot out-give God. When you lay down your treasure, God responds.

True worship is at the place of painful sacrifice, where both the cherished and the precious are laid down. Nobody can help you build this altar on which you must sacrifice your all. Nobody will arrange the wood for you and nobody will help bind that sacrifice of yours. It must come on your volition. As you get ready to build an altar of sacrifice in your life know that he who withholds nothing from God has everything God can offer. If you give God your precious gift, He gives you His precious gift. God's all can only come in return for a man's all. God's treasury is opened to those who have laid down their treasures at the foot of the cross.

## Will you let go the precious?

God needs your all, no matter how small it is, it will make all the difference. It brought breakthrough in the realm of provision for the widow at Zarephath when she let go her precious all to meet the need of the man of God, Elijah.

It took *"except a little oil"* for the prophet's widow to experience a miracle.

It took someone's *"five loaves and two small fish"* for five thousand to be fed.

## When should you raise altars?

1. (1) When you receive new revelations, seal them up with raised altars. (See Genesis 26:25, Genesis 35:1 & 7).
    When God revealed Himself to Isaac, he sealed his experience by raising an altar of prayer.
    When God revealed Himself to Jacob, he raised an altar there unto God.
2. When God shows you His favor, raise an altar unto Him (See Genesis 33:20). God showed Jacob favor before his brother Esau, and he raised an altar unto God.
3. When you experience victory over the enemy in your life, raise an altar unto God. (See Exodus 17:15).
    When Moses experienced victory over the Amalekites, he raised an altar unto the Lord and called it "The Lord is my banner". Actually this altar was also raised to set God in a continuous battle against the Amalekites.
4. When you want God to war against the enemies in your life (See Exodus 17:15 & 16).
5. When you feel pressed on every side, raise an altar of sacrifice so as to turn the tides. Do you remember the heathen King? (2 Kings 3)

# CHAPTER 12

## Don't Get It All Wrong, God Is Not Indifferent

- Does no one seem to hear your cry?
- Are the castles you constructed now crumbled over you?
- Has the ground where you build proven to be mire?
- Are your secret dreams and hopes perishing in the grave of time?
- Do the heavens above you seem to be iron and bronze?

Do you think your God has forsaken you and has become indifferent to what is happening to you? If that is what you think, then you' have got it all wrong. The God we are talking about is too big to play games with anybody, He is too faithful to fail and above all He is not indifferent to your situation. His word says, *"yet the Lord longs to be gracious to you, He rises to show you compassion. For the LORD is a God of justice. Blessed are all who wait for Him!"* (Isaiah 30:18).

God is not indifferent to all that is happening to you. He is not indifferent to your frustration. He is not indifferent to your needs. He is not indifferent to all that has caused you pains and tears. He longs to be gracious to you. To long means to earnestly desire or to want something. God longs to show you His infinite tenderness and compassions. He longs to show you His favor. In fact He is taking steps to help; He wants to be and is already a part of your suffering. About the Israelites, He said:

> *"… 'I have indeed seen the misery of my people in Egypt. I have heard them crying out because of their slave drivers, and I am concerned about their suffering. So I have come down to rescue them from the hand of the Egyptians and to bring them up out of that land into a good and spacious land, a land flowing with milk and honey--the home of the Canaanites, Hittites, Amorites, Perizzites, Hivites and Jebusites.'"* (Exodus 3:7-8a)

- God has seen your misery.
- God has heard you crying.
- God is concerned about your suffering.
- God has roused Himself on your behalf.

Do you feel there is something holding you back? Do you feel you are operating under some oppressive power?

> *"I will say to the north, 'Give them up!' and to the south, 'Do not hold them back.' Bring my sons from afar and my daughters from the ends of the earth-everyone who is called by my name, whom I created for my glory, whom I formed and made." (Isaiah 43:6, 7).*

God is interested to see His children released from whatever has held them bound and wherever they have been held bound. He is commanding your release so you can be free for Him. His longing too is for those who are far from Him to come home. Yes, for everyone called by His Name, created for His glory, and formed and made by Him. That includes you!

You were formed to be a *"glory-bearer"* and anything that deprives you of that does not please God. Forget the former things: the former difficulties, failures, lack etc. Forget even the former victories. Too much concentration on the past deprives you of new visions. Too much concentration on things that have happened can render you totally oblivious of things that are happening. The secret is to keep your eyes on Him and to wait for Him.

## You are worth more than things

Our world has established a lie for a long time and there are many who profess the Name of Christ yet are caught in this web of deception from the pit of hell. People have been made to think that a man's worth is determined by the things he or she owns. The Lord Jesus Christ said, *"A man's life does not consist in the abundance of his possession"* (See Luke 12:15). It is man who gives value to things and not things giving man his value. God says, *"I will make man more precious than fine gold; even a man than the golden Wedge of Ophir."* (Isaiah 13:12, KJV)

Man has brought himself so low that things seem to have more value than man. How do you value your brethren? How do you value your spouse? How do you value your friends? By the things they possess? How will you treat a friend, child, brother, or spouse who damages something of yours? It is a shame that man will make something and then value it more than his own life or the life of a fellow human. Why on earth will someone take the life of another for the sake of material things? Why on earth would someone put his own very life in jeopardy for the sake of things?

God has a plan of restoration, to restore man's lost value to something that cannot be bought with a price, not even the price of finest gold. In fact He has already done that; you are worth the price of the life of the eternal Christ and Lord, Jesus. That is the value, which was paid for your redemption.

- Your conscience is worth the life of Jesus; you cannot afford to sell it again at whatever price

- Your body is worth the life of Jesus, you cannot afford to degrade it. What gives you value is not what you have or who you are but whose you are. You are the child of the Most High God. You are worth more than the purest gold, a billion times more. Do not allow the world get you caught in this web of deception. Your worth is in your God. Value nothing else. Do not join the rat race, it's not worth it.

## What matters is that which God says

As a Christian you have a new frame of reference from which everything is viewed, judged or measured. In this world in which you and I live, things are viewed, judged and measured on their frame of reference which is different from ours - God's eyes. When we endeavor to do things through the eyes of God (In light of His eternal Word and the witness of His Spirit within) things or people, which might otherwise be viewed as meaningless, useless and a total failure, will be seen with a whole new meaning and value.

In that which you are doing, you may appear in the eyes of man to have failed, even in your own eyes, but in the eyes of God you are a total success. Maybe somehow, somewhere you abandoned a more gorgeous vocation or business opportunity or just anything else which may appear to be a success to those *"who matter"* in your life but you have abandoned for the sake of what you believe is God's call for your life and now nothing seems working. You look back in regret and disappointment. I want to tell you that success in the sight of God consist in doing what God wants you to do, where He wants you to do it, how He wants you to do it, when He wants you to do it. That is what success really is. Success does not consist in how quick the results are got, it does not consist in how gorgeous the results are but in that which God validates and accepts. Think of it!

Will the world have considered our glorious Lord Jesus Christ to have succeeded? Certainly not! They saw Him as a failure, as one who could not even save Himself from the cruelty of death on a cross. They saw Him as one who died in the prime of life. But how did the Father see Him? The very fact that you and I proclaim His Name, more than 2000 years later shows the grandeur of the life He lived on earth, the victory He won on the cross of Calvary and the triumph He brought by His resurrection. Where the world thought He had failed is the very place where the greatest victory of any battle ever fought was won.

What about Paul the apostle? Will the world have considered him a success? Certainly not! He had abandoned his successful religious profession as a

Pharisee to become the *"ring leader of a sect called the Way"* and was labelled as insane. In the eyes of the world, the very fact that he was in chains meant he had failed already. But in the eyes of God Paul did not fail he was a success. The good thing about it is that both our Lord and Paul saw themselves and their mission through the eyes of the Father. That is why as his life on earth drew to a close, He could say

> *"Father, the time has come. Glorify your Son, that your Son may glorify you. For you granted him authority over all people that he might give eternal life to all those you have given him. Now this is eternal life: that they may know you, the only true God, and Jesus Christ, whom you have sent. I have brought you glory on earth by completing the work you gave me to do. And now, Father, glorify me in your presence with the glory I had with you before the world began. "I have revealed you to those whom you gave me out of the world. They were yours; you gave them to me and they have obeyed your word.* (John 17:1-6)

Paul also could say

> *"I have fought the good fight, I have finished the race, I have kept the faith. Now there is in store for me the crown of righteousness, which the Lord, the righteous Judge, will award to me on that day--and not only to me, but also to all who have longed for his appearing."* (2 Timothy 4:7-8).

**Eternal Values**

Like I said in the last section, the world has its own frame of reference from the believer. With them things are measured by what can be accomplished now. Things that can make the greatest money now, things that can give the greatest pleasure now, things that can give the greatest satisfaction now, and things that can give the greatest recognition now. All such things are given the greatest value and worth by the world. As a believer, we look at the worth of things with respect to their eternal value.

Listen to what the apostle Paul had to say,

> *"Therefore we do not lose heart. Though outwardly we are wasting away, yet inwardly we are being renewed day by day. For our light and momentary troubles are achieving for us eternal glory that far outweighs them all. So we fix our eyes not on what is seen, but on what is unseen. For what is seen is temporary, but what is unseen is eternal."* (2Corinthians 4:16-18)

Outwardly you may seem to be losing everything. Outwardly you may seem to be failing. Outwardly you may seem to be wasting your life, wasting your time and resources. But inwardly it is totally different. There is an inner witness of approval and assurance from the Spirit of Grace that what matters is receiving the attention it deserves.

Whatever we suffer here on earth for the sake of integrity, truth, holiness and the gospel of Christ, the Bible describes as light and momentary. And indeed compared with the eternal glory they are achieving for us, they can just and should just be considered as light and momentary. Continue to sow into eternity; it is the place where the harvest is sure to be preserved.

# CHAPTER 13

## Keep Holding On

The phrase "keep holding on" could be given many interpretations. However, whatever interpretation may be given it suggests a build-up of courage to continue doing something in the face of fading strength and other resources.

What do you do when all around you is fading? When conflict is rising all about you? When you are left alone in the face of adversity? When there is just nothing visible you can lean on? *"When your trusted watchers fly"*? *"When your secret hopes have perished in the grave of years gone by"*?

I tell you, keep holding on, do not give up. Do not give in.

**Storm drove him to the place of abundance**

I want us to learn a lesson from someone who held on in the face of rising adversity and immense conflict. It happened to Isaac.

Please read Genesis 26:1-6, 12-34.

Here we find a situation of famine in the land of Gerar. God asks Isaac to stay in Gerar rather than move to Egypt. A famine is great lack of something. God asked Isaac to stay in the midst of famine because He wanted to teach Isaac that what matters is not the condition of the environment but being where God wants you to be. At any moment in your life you should be able to ask *"Am I where God wants me to be?"* For Isaac to have attempted to go down to Egypt, it meant he already felt a pinch of the famine. In obeying God to stay in Gerar, somehow, he was to continue to feel, the effect of the famine. Why Abraham was called to *"step out in faith"*, Isaac was called to "stay in faith'. He was asked to hold on in the midst of fading economic resources and his obedience brought about his blessing.

Your blessing is not in the world system, not in the green pastures of this world but in where God wants you to be, even in the famine stricken Gerar. I am not saying we shouldn't seek for a better living; all I am saying is, never seek for a better living at the expense of God's command to you, with respect to your geographical location. What did Isaac do in the midst of the famine? He sowed a seed. There must be something for God to bless so that it multiplies and that must be a seed sown, not one kept on a shelf.

Caution! Anyone who wants to be at peace with his enemies does not need God's blessings. Anyone who wants to be loved and cherished by his enemies does not need God's blessings. When God begins to bless, the enemies get frightened, and He always does it in a way that will be evident. The blessings of God make a clear demarcation between your friends and your enemies. People, who are happy seeing you in your state of poverty, want and disease will become hostile when God brings into your life His supernatural blessing. When God blesses, your abilities become the match for entire groups or communities of people, Isaac was more than a match to Abimelech and his entire nation.

If there's one thing you should get out of this passage, it is that disputes and opposition are just moving you to a God-encounter that will change your life. When Isaac's servants dug a well over which the men of Gerar quarrelled, they did not stop digging. Keep digging, keep investing and you will soon find the right well, you will soon reap the harvest. From disputes (Esek) and opposition (Sinar), Isaac moved to a specious place where he could flourish all the more. Your problems are pushing you to a spacious place for God's blessings to take a new dimension. Problems are only there to create room for you to flourish. You know the well Isaac finally found was called Beersheba, meaning well of seven. The well was seven times the capacity of any other well he had ever found. God is taking you to a spacious place through your trials, so as to expand, promote and propel you to your destiny.

Do you know the hostility of Abimelech's men actually paved the path for Isaac's God-encounter? (see verse 23-24)

Another lesson I want you to get out of this passage; never leave until you are sent away by the person who matters. The opposition from the Philistines towards Isaac did not cause Isaac to leave their land. He continued to prosper in spite of the increasing hostility. Stay in the place God had asked you to.

Isaac did not leave Gerar until Abimelech drove him away (verse 16). Do not leave your place of duty and responsibility unless the person who matters says you should.

Thirdly, note that God was with Isaac throughout; before the famine, during the famine, and after the famine; He was with him always.

## The need for tenacity

*"You need to persevere so that when you have done the will of God you will receive what he has promised." (Hebrews 10:36)*

Isaac never gave up his search for the wells in spite of the continuous opposition from the people around. In spite of the fading circumstances that surrounded him, he held on to his purpose. There is need to be tenacious in the face of storms, when all seems hopeless, when you feel abandoned and forgotten, despised and forsaken, hold on to your pursuit. Does not the Word of God say *"you need to persevere so that when you have done the will of God, you will receive what He had promised"* (Hebrews 10:36)? Perseverance is what you need to keep on doing the will of God, which eventually leads to inheriting the promises of God. Why perseverance? Because *"perseverance must finish its work so that you may be mature and complete, not lacking anything."* (James 1:4).

Thus tenacity will lead to

1. Maturity
2. Completeness
3. Fulfilment.

You and I need to attain a degree of maturity to be able to inherit certain promises of God and even the things we desire so much. Resolve henceforth to be tenacious, to persevere no matter the circumstances or people opposing you.

Tenacity keeps any adversary at a distance. The devil and his host are afraid of people who hold on and refuse to give up or give in. Let there be a firm resolve in your mind to press on even when all hope seems to have faded like morning mist in sunlight, when all seems to have flown away like soap bubbles in the wind. Hold on and press on, then you shall reap the harvest of perseverance.

## Do not hasten

It can be very tempting to make hasty decisions when all seems fading and there is no light rising in the horizon, no cloud symbolic of rain in a dry and thirsty land. The decisions we take whether wholeheartedly or half-heartedly in times of crises are usually far reaching than we may ever anticipate.

> *"So Isaac called for Jacob and blessed him and commanded him: "Do not marry a Canaanite woman. Go at once to Paddan Aram, to the house of your mother's father Bethuel. Take a wife for yourself there, from among the daughters of Laban, your mother's brother. May God Almighty bless you and make you fruitful and increase your numbers until you become a community of peoples. May he give you and your descendants the blessing given to*

> *Abraham, so that you may take possession of the land where you now live as an alien, the land God gave to Abraham." Then Isaac sent Jacob on his way, and he went to Paddan Aram, to Laban son of Bethuel the Aramean, the brother of Rebekah, who was the mother of Jacob and Esau.*
>
> *Now Esau learned that Isaac had blessed Jacob and had sent him to Paddan Aram to take a wife from there, and that when he blessed him he commanded him, "Do not marry a Canaanite woman," and that Jacob had obeyed his father and mother and had gone to Paddan Aram. Esau then realized how displeasing the Canaanite women were to his father Isaac; so he went to Ishmael and married Mahalath, the sister of Nebaioth and daughter of Ishmael son of Abraham, in addition to the wives he already had." (Genesis 28:1-9)*

As I said earlier, there are actions and decisions which when taken will influence more people than the actor himself. Decisions you take do not affect you alone, though at the moment of taking the decision it may appear thus. Esau's decision to marry Hittite women, affected his mother's welfare, he could only realize the consequences when it was too late. The extent of the damage of any decision can never be truly weighed before the act.

Do you make decisions independent of those who matter, who will be affected directly or indirectly? Know that the consequences of each compromise and conformity cannot be reversed. You see, the truth is that every decision, at the time it is made looks wise and good to him who is making the decision. That is why there is need to consult your spiritual authorities or counsellors who are able to judge independently the correctness of your decision. Esau's fundamental problem was independence, the failure and refusal to seek the opinion of another, especially his authorities. May it not be your portion!

## Rest for the night

> *"Jacob left Beersheba and set out for Haran. When he reached a certain place, he stopped for the night because the sun had set..."* (Genesis 28:10-18).

When it is night in your life; when the sun has set; when there is no more light on your path; stop and rest for the night. *"When he reached a certain place…"* It is true that the places where we need to stop are usually unanticipated and unknown to us; they always seem to be places of no importance which pose the greatest hindrance. We encounter many of such places on this spiritual journey, when the night falls. At such moments wisdom demands that you stop for the night even if at that place "your rest is a stone".

Stopping for the night is not giving up, neither is it equivalent to retreating. It is better to endure the pain of resting your head on a stone than the wreckage, which results from continuing in the dark. In times of waiting, in times of resting for the night, God will always speak. Nightfall is an opportunity to listen to and hear the voice of God. It is a time to seek God's face and will anew, to get His direction, His approval or disapproval. Do not hurry in the dark, but halt and wait for the dawn. As long as there is a sunset, there must be a sunrise, as you wait, expect the sun to rise.

Between God and you, is just a staircase for you to climb. Nightfall is divine providence for God-encounter-moments for you to listen, observe and anticipate. It is a moment of revelation. God is right where you are, in the circumstance you find yourself, though you may not be aware; the nightfall is to bring you to a state of total awareness of His presence. Awareness of His presence leads to reverence and worship.

## There is always a morning

> *"Early the next morning Jacob took the same stone he had placed under his head and set it up as a pillar and poured oil on top of it… Then Jacob continued on his journey and came to the land of the eastern peoples."* (Genesis 28:18 - Genesis 29:10).

Does the night seem so long? Does it seem you will have to wait endlessly? After every night, there is always a morning, there is always a sunrise after every sunset as long as the fixed laws of heaven and earth remain in place. What makes the difference is whether you met with God in your night or not. A

God-encounter will transform every Luz (turning aside) to a Bethel (House of God). It takes you from a state of unawareness of His presence and favor to a state of awareness. Wait for the dawn, the assurance of the light of His presence. Every dawn comes with an anointing to worship, for it brings a new sense of the presence of the creator. Jacob only continued his journey when it was dawn. Do not attempt to continue before the light of God has risen. The morning will take you to a new sphere of commitment to the God of heaven.

**Wait and keep waiting**

No matter how long the night may seem, please wait and keep waiting, make no haste, my friend, make no haste in spite of the pressure and pain the night may bring, open the eyes of your heart and see Him there with you.

Let us see the dangers of taking a step in the dark.

> "*Then they moved on from Bethel. While they were still some distance from Ephrath, Rachel began to give birth and had great difficulty. And as she was having great difficulty in childbirth, the midwife said to her, "Don't be afraid, for you have another son." As she breathed her last--for she was dying--she named her son Ben-Oni. But his father named him Benjamin. So Rachel died and was buried on the way to Ephrath (that is, Bethlehem). Over her tomb Jacob set up a pillar, and to this day that pillar marks Rachel's tomb. Israel moved on again and pitched his tent beyond Migdal Eder.*" (Genesis 35:16 - 21)

The instructions God gave Jacob in Gen 35: 1 were clear. He was to go to Bethel and settle there, in the place of worship prayer and sacrifice. God did not ask Jacob to visit Bethel for a season but to make it his habitation. We find nowhere in scripture, a record of God asking Jacob to move from Bethel but as we read in verse 16, for whatever reason, Jacob carried his family away from Bethel.

When a man decides to move away from God's presence for whatever reason, he can only expose himself to danger and calamity, pain, sorrow and loss.

Note that Bethel was a place of

1. Revelation - verse 7 and verse 9
2. Transformation - verse 10
3. Conversation (Communion) - verse 11
4. Worship - verse 14
5. Covenants - Genesis 28:20-22

There are two reasons, I believe, why Jacob moved from Bethel, without God's instruction:

- The pain and discomfort of the place of transformation
- The spirit of wandering that was in his family line.

What lessons can we draw from there?

1. Never move away from where God has asked you to settle or from what He asked you to do without a clear instruction from Him.
2. Do not abandon the place of your transformation no matter how painful it may seem
3. You must deal ruthlessly with negative generational traits in order that they may have no influence on you.
4. Unless you are willing to endure the pain that comes with transformation and conformity to His likeness, you can never make His presence your dwelling.

What were the consequences of this move from "The House of God"?

Jacob exposed his family to the devil;

1. He lost his wife (verse 19);
2. His son lost the fear of God and slept with one of Jacob's wives (verse 22).
3. He became a restless wanderer (verse 21 and 27).

If you do not settle your mind on what God wants you to do and where he wants you to be, the spirit of wandering and purposelessness will take hold of you because nothing else and no other place will give meaning to life.

From the moment Jacob carried his family away from where God wanted him to be (House of God), there was no longer

- Any revelation of God's person
- Any communion with God
- Any worship of God.

Besides, his children became wild.

If your life is void of revelations of God's glory, void of communion with God, void of true worship, then ask yourself if you are where God wants you to be doing what He wants you to do.

Has your night been too long? Has the sky over you been grey all along? Do not leave your Bethel.

## You can hasten the dawn

> "Is it not to share your food with the hungry and to provide the poor wanderer with shelter-- when you see the naked, to clothe him, and not to turn away from your own flesh and blood? Then your light will break forth like the dawn, and your healing will quickly appear; then your righteousness will go before you, and the glory of the LORD will be your rear guard. Then you will call, and the LORD will answer; you will cry for help, and he will say: Here am I. "If you do away with the yoke of oppression, with the pointing finger and malicious talk, and if you spend yourselves in behalf of the hungry and satisfy the needs of the oppressed, then your light will rise in the darkness, and your night will become like the noonday." (Isaiah 58: 7-10)

Most often the night seems dark and unnecessarily long when all one thinks of is himself. Self-centeredness delays the dawn. Do you want to hasten your dawn? Then an attitude of surrendering, sacrifice and selflessness will do the following:-

1. Cause your light to break forth like the dawn, verse 8.
2. Your healing will quickly appear, verse 8
3. Your righteousness will go before you, verse 8
4. The glory of the Lord will be your guard, verse 8
5. Your light will rise in the darkness. Verse 10
6. Your night will become like the noonday verse 10.

Will you lift up your eyes beyond you and be involved in the welfare of another? Will you stretch your resources to include the need of another?

Surrendering, sacrifice and selflessness dispel the night and brings forth the light. They dispel the clouds blocking your sunshine. They turn your night to noonday. At noon, the shadows are at the minimum, thus anything that can block your view is reduced to the minimum. You see the real things and not shadows. Spend to shelter someone. Spend on another's behalf. Satisfy someone else's hunger.

Make no further delay, you can hasten the dawn and cause your sun to rise. You can dispel your night and change your darkness into light. Hallelujah!

# Chapter 14

## Overcoming Loneliness

Nothing frustrates like the feeling of loneliness. Aloneness and loneliness are quite different. A man can be lonely in a crowd of a thousand people. The fundamental difference between loneliness and aloneness is that loneliness brings a feeling of frustration while aloneness brings feelings of fulfilment. Not everyone found alone is lonely and not everyone found in a crowd has company. The greatest loneliness is that experienced by someone who has everything but no one with whom to share. This feeling of loneliness can take a total hold of a man or woman, boy or girl in situations where all seems fading.

**Be a Well**

*"Then Jacob continued on his journey and came to the land of the eastern peoples. There he saw a well in the field, with three flocks of sheep lying near it because the flocks were watered from that well. The stone over the mouth of the well was large. When all the flocks were gathered there, the shepherds would roll the stone away from the well's mouth and water the sheep. Then they would return the stone to its place over the mouth of the well."* (Genesis 29:1-3)

The only reason the flocks gathered round that point is because of the presence of the well from which their need for water could be satisfied, where their thirst could be quenched. There are too many people in our world thirsty for the water of life. Countless are thirsty for love and will gather around who ever will meet their need. Draw out from the well of love God has placed in you to satisfy the need of those around you. Remember there are springs of living water flowing within your belly from which others can drink. People will gather around what can refresh them. Do you want people to gather round you? Do you want to overcome loneliness? Then get out of your world. Break the shell around you and be involved in the lives of others in a positive manner. I want you to understand that you have something to offer:

- You can make someone happy
- You can make someone feel safe
- You can put a smile on someone's face
- You can meet the needs of someone
- You can be a channel of someone's joy
- You can be a channel of someone's hope
- You can be a channel of someone's comfort
- You can be a channel of blessings for someone
- You can be a channel of encouragement for someone
- You can become the channel of healing for someone
- You can become the channel of deliverance for someone
- You can become the channel of freedom and salvation for some; holding out the lifeline of life.

You know, the well had water in it but could have been permanently sealed. This well could have been difficult to open (rolling away the stone) thus making it not useful. Many people are lonely and frustrated because they have permanently locked up the deposit of God in them, which could be used in blessing others. Have you been too difficult for the Spirit of God to open up to bless others? Is there a stone over your well? As Jacob rolled away the stone from that well, God will roll away the stone from the mouth of your well to water the sheep of Jesus, those in the fold and those out of the fold. Your stone is being rolled away so that you can become a blessing to the people around you.

- Will you surrender your pride to the Lord?
- Will you carry your cross and follow Him today?
- Will you spend yourself for another?

## You too can blossom

> *"In days to come Jacob will take root, Israel will bud and blossom and fill all the world with fruit."* (Isaiah 27: 6)

I want you to take note of something from the above verse; it is Jacob who takes root but Israel blossoms. Jacob is the old man while Israel is the new man. Jacob is the unbroken unbended man while Israel is the broken and limping man. Now, when a tree blossoms, what happens?

- It produces flowers, which beautify the environment
- It produces a fragrance, which attracts bees, butterflies and little birds to feed on the nectar. I believe as the bees and birds feed on the nectar of the blossomed plant, the plant enjoys the sweet melodies they make.

Permit me ask you a question or more:

Whose world are you beautifying? Who are you making to breathe easier? Who are you struggling to *"give a better life"*? Will you bud and blossom?

You can overcome loneliness.

The Bible says, *"Many curry favor with a ruler and everyone is the friend of a man who gives gifts"* (Proverbs 19:6). Will you begin to sacrifice for others? If you do, loneliness will fly away like morning midst.

## Love life to live happily

> *"So Jacob served seven years to get Rachel, but they seemed like only a few days to him because of his love for her. Then Jacob said to Laban,*

> *"Give me my wife. My time is completed, and I want to lie with her."*
> (Genesis 29:20-21)

Jacob had fallen in love with the girl of his life when he decided to work for seven years as bride price. The Bible says those seven years where to him like a few days. Now what was the secret to this happy labor? His love for Rachel. To live happily you must love life. Love life in order to enjoy your labor though it seems to be difficult. There's no extent of sacrifice to which love cannot stretch. Love whatever you are doing and time will mean nothing.

> Seven years seemed like a few days. If you will love life then,
> Seven years of waiting will seem like a few days
> Seven years of pain will seem like a few days
> Seven years of suffering will seem like a few days
> Seven years of service will seem like a few years.

Love has the capacity to diminish the odds. If you love life you will settle for nothing but the best - the abundance of life Christ came to give. Jacob's goal was to have Rachel. The number of years of investment to attain his goal mattered little to him. When you love your vision, when you love your goal, the price to pay becomes insignificant. To successfully attain your vision, to live happily take your eyes off the investment and price you must make and focus on the goal.

You must know what you want out of life and go for it wholeheartedly, settling for nothing else. Jacob did not settle for Leah because his goal was Rachel and not just a wife. The one who has not made up his mind will settle for anything life offers. You can get what you want out of life in spite of the circumstances.

Jacob set his mind, his heart and emotions on nothing else but Rachel - his goal - and no substitute could bring him satisfaction, not even Leah who was of the same parents as Rachel. Decide to settle for nothing but your vision. You must set your whole heart, your whole mind and your whole feelings on that which you must accomplish. Moreover, tradition did not stop Jacob from realizing his dream - Rachel.

Be willing to get beyond the bounds of tradition to accomplish your destiny. Not even an additional seven years of work was too big a price to pay. How do you esteem your vision? How do you value life? Everything else, even the price fades in the site of a highly esteemed vision. Go in for the full price; do not expect anything to happen until the full price has been paid. Pay the price for a happy life, and overcome loneliness.

# CHAPTER 15

## When God Breaks Into Your World

Sometimes one may just accept to live with a particular situation. Too many people settle for what is not supposed to be theirs. They seem to have accepted what life offers rather than going for the best they can get out of life. For such, there are times God, in His omniscience and omnipotence, decides to break into their world to bring a change. Why do I use the word *"break"*? Because they seem to have shut God out of the situation in which they are found, as a result of unholy contentment *"on the wrong side of life"*.

> Are you one of such?
> Have you settled for just a substitute of what is due you?
> Have you made your home in the wilderness?
> God will break in to bring a change.

### Breaking life's limits

> *"One day Peter and John were going up to the temple at the time of prayer-- at three in the afternoon. Now a man crippled from birth was being carried to the temple gate called Beautiful, where he was put every day to beg from those going into the temple courts. When he saw Peter and John about to enter, he asked them for money. Peter looked straight at him, as did John.*

> *Then Peter said, "Look at us!" So the man gave them his attention, expecting to get something from them. Then Peter said, "Silver or gold I do not have, but what I have I give you. In the name of Jesus Christ of Nazareth, walk." Taking him by the right hand, he helped him up, and instantly the man's feet and ankles became strong. He jumped to his feet and began to walk. Then he went with them into the temple courts, walking and jumping, and praising God. When all the people saw him walking and praising God, 10they recognized him as the same man who used to sit begging at the temple gate called Beautiful, and they were filled with wonder and amazement at what had happened to him."* (Acts 3:1-10).

This crippled man had a natural limitation unable to walk on his own. He perpetually depended for his welfare. He had to be carried by others to gate Beautiful daily to beg. The Bible says, everyday he had a cycle which he followed; his house (if at all he had any of his own) to the gate and back to the house. His sphere of interaction was limited by what life offered him. Remember, in those days anyone with such a physical defect was not allowed into the temple. The gate was as far as he could go, the doors where closed to him. Surely he saw the beauty and magnificence of the Temple from the gate and even desired to enter. He saw others walk pass him every day to the place that was the dream of every Jew but nature's limitations could not allow him. The circumstances of life had reduced him to a beggar whose life was a meaningless routine of complete dependence on the mercy of others.

What limitations have life placed on you? Have you been confined to a meaningless routine by the circumstances in which you find yourself? Daily, you see others walk in and out of the same place you will really like to enter but cannot. Have the circumstances of life made you a complete dependant in some areas of your life? Have the circumstances in life made you a complete financial dependant? You seek to have your financial independence but it just seems impossible.

Have the circumstances in life made you a total emotional dependant? You seek to have some emotional independence but are not able?

Have the circumstances in life made you a total social dependent? You seek *"social independence"* but cannot get it? Just as this crippled man sat in front of an open gate but could not enter, there are many sitting or standing before open doors but are unable to enter into the place of their dreams. Why? Because of the limitations of nature or circumstances; poverty, ill health and curses! That is not where God wants you to be. You may have accepted it because of unholy contentment but God wants you out of that box of meaningless routine of complete dependence. He wants to take away that limitation. My friend, you too can live above or beyond life's limitations. The Bible says, *"one day Peter and John…"* One day, God broke into his world to bring about a change and extend his borders. Someone has called that *"a blind date with destiny"*. God can bring meaning into that routine.

Let us digress a bit from the cripple to the apostles Peter and John. The Bible says they were going up to the temple at the time of prayer. This talks of discipline. Those who are to influence the world must have learned the art of discipline. They must have learned to give time to the important things of life. These are people with established priorities in life. There is no greater blessing than that of an organized life, with priorities in place. Though Peter and John had a purpose, they observed their environment carefully. They could read the desires and expectations of this beggar. Focus is good but do not fail to notice the pains, needs, desires and longings of the people around you. An attitude of love and concern will go a long you to give God an opportunity to break into their world of suffering. We all need a careful balance of focused priorities and observance of the things around i.e. a careful balance of "work and play" and, only the Spirit of God can work that in us.

*"Peter looked straight at him…"* It is time the saints begin looking straight at their obstacles and address them with the Word of God.

Many people may be expecting from you that which you cannot offer, just as this beggar expected silver and gold from the apostles. It is time we let people know what we can offer. Do not attempt to meet every need; the truth is that you cannot. Like the apostles, be honest with yourself to say *"this or that I do not have but what I do have I give you"*.

Begin to use what you have for the glory of God. Do not be limited by what you do not have. Life is meant to be lived and enjoyed with what you have and not by what you expect to have. Just as the apostles offered this man what they had and brought him out of his limitation, you too can offer somebody what you have to bring him out of his limitation. You can use just what you have to be involved positively in the lives of others. You do not need other things.

Coming back to the crippled beggar, his expectations where tied to the silver or gold the apostles could offer him. He had no thought of ever receiving his miracle of healing. He had no thought of anything beyond a coin or two, but received what far outweighed his expectations. The Bible says God is able to do beyond what we expect.

> *"Now to him who is able to do immeasurably more than all we ask or imagine, according to his power that is at work within us,"* (Ephesians 3: 20)

Immeasurably more than you can ask or imagine! Is that not great? Is that not awesome? Isn't that grace abundant and amazing? Will you not raise up those holy hands and bless His holy Name? That is the God you serve! In a nanosecond, He can make all things new. He can restore hope and joy when all seemed to have faded.

Those same ankles which could not carry him could now carry him. His weakness became his strength. His failures were turned to success. His limits were removed and he could now walk into the Temple courts and into the Temple itself - the dream of every Jew of his time. This same man who could not stand was now able to jump. His song changed from *"I beg"* to *"praise the Lord"*. He changed from a position of pity and empathy to one of admiration by others in the place he would otherwise never have entered.

God is about making you a source of wonder and amazement as a result of His working in your life. You shall be able to walk into that open door God will place before you. He will surely bring about your financial independence. He will surely bring about your emotional independence and extend your sphere of influence. What makes the difference is that God decides to break into your world.

## From Lodebar to Jerusalem

The God you serve brings surprises to his children; those who wait on Him and those who have given up. Do you know another such person who had given up? There is one in the Bible called Mephibosheth.

> *"David asked, "Is there anyone still left of the house of Saul to whom I can show kindness for Jonathan's sake?" Now there was a servant of Saul's household named Ziba. They called him to appear before David, and the king said to him, "Are you Ziba?" "Your servant," he replied. The king asked, "Is there no one still left of the house of Saul to whom I can show God's kindness?" Ziba answered the king, "There is still a son of Jonathan; he is crippled in both feet." "Where is he?" the king asked. Ziba answered, "He is at the house of Makir son of Ammiel in Lo Debar." So King David had him brought from Lo Debar, from the house of Makir son of Ammiel. When Mephibosheth son of Jonathan, the son of Saul, came to David, he bowed down to pay him honor.*
> *David said, "Mephibosheth!" "Your servant," he replied. "Don't be afraid," David said to him, "for I will surely show you kindness for the sake of your father Jonathan. I will restore to you all the land that belonged to your grandfather Saul, and you will always eat at my table." Mephibosheth bowed down and said, "What is your servant, that you should notice a dead dog like me?" Then the king summoned Ziba, Saul's servant, and said to him, "I have given your master's grandson everything that belonged to Saul and his family. You and your sons and your servants are to farm the land for him and bring in the crops, so that your master's grandson may be provided for. And Mephibosheth, grandson of your master, will always eat at my table." (Now Ziba had fifteen sons and twenty servants.) Then Ziba said to the king, "Your servant will do whatever my lord the king commands his servant to do." So Mephibosheth ate at David's table like one of the king's sons. Mephibosheth had a young son named Mica, and all the members of Ziba's household were servants of Mephibosheth. And Mephibosheth lived in*

*Jerusalem, because he always ate at the king's table, and he was crippled in both feet." (2 Samuel 9:1-13)*

Here is another person Mephibosheth, who had resigned into what life offered him. He had accepted the dictates of the circumstances he found himself in as a result of his family line. But God decided to break into his world and bring a change. Mephibosheth was at Lodebar, which means *"no pasture"*, he was contented with the wrong side of life, dwelling in a place which offered nothing.

Have you decided to settle at Lodebar, a place of no spiritual pasture, nothing to cultivate? As Mephibosheth was fished out of his hiding place of resignation, God will pull you out into the *"city of God"* - Jerusalem. He will bring you to feed on His table. Do not continue to see yourself as a dead dog. No matter where you are, you remain a prince or a princess of the Most High. When He breaks into your world, unknown to you, He will bring about a total restoration of all what you lost. The blood covenant between God and you compels Him to break into your world and bring a restoration. Hallelujah!

# Chapter 16

## Teaching You Dependence

From when Eve was deceived and Adam defiantly transgressed God's law, man has always sought independence from God. The tendency of the average human being is to shut God out completely and make independent decisions. Man constantly seeks to provide for himself what he really cannot. His first attempt was to cloth himself and this met with total failure as even his well-designed dress failed to provide a complete coverage of his nakedness and to provide the needed warmth. It needed God's intervention for the things to be put right. (See Genesis 3:7 and 22).

This tendency of independence from God has made man a constant loser, who fails to experience the best God intents. God's desire has been for us to depend on Him, to look up to Him so as to enjoy the best He has in store. In His love and mercy towards us He constantly creates circumstances that will strip us of our arrogance and bring us to a point of total dependence and trust.

**He did it to Israel**

> "*Remember how the LORD your God led you all the way in the desert these forty years, to humble you and to test you in order to know what was in your heart, whether or not you would keep his commands. He humbled you,*

> *causing you to hunger and then feeding you with manna, which neither you nor your fathers had known, to teach you that man does not live on bread alone but on every word that comes from the mouth of the LORD. Your clothes did not wear out and your feet did not swell during these forty years. Know then in your heart that as a man disciplines his son, so the LORD your God disciplines you."*
>
> *"When you have eaten and are satisfied, praise the LORD your God for the good land he has given you. Be careful that you do not forget the LORD your God, failing to observe his commands, his laws and his decrees that I am giving you this day. Otherwise, when you eat and are satisfied, when you build fine houses and settle down, and when your herds and flocks grow large and your silver and gold increase and all you have is multiplied, then your heart will become proud and you will forget the LORD your God, who brought you out of Egypt, out of the land of slavery. He led you through the vast and dreadful desert, that thirsty and waterless land, with its venomous snakes and scorpions. He brought you water out of hard rock. He gave you manna to eat in the desert, something your fathers had never known, to humble and to test you so that in the end it might go well with you. You may say to yourself, "My power and the strength of my hands have produced this wealth for me." But remember the LORD your God, for it is he who gives you the ability to produce wealth, and so confirms his covenant, which he swore to your forefathers, as it is today."* (Deuteronomy 8: 2-5, 10-18).

The sovereign Lord took Israel through the wilderness journey in order to teach them dependence on Him; The Bible says He did the following in order to humble them.

- He led them through the desert
- He caused them to hunger and then fed them.
- He took them through a waterless desert and provided water for them from a rock.

Why? In order to teach them the following lessons:

- That man does not live on bread alone but on every word that comes from the mouth of the Lord (verse 3).

- That God can do miracles and meet their basic needs (verse 4).
- That they may understand that He treats them as sons (verse 5).
- That it is He who gives the ability to produce wealth (verse 18)

Could God have taken Israel into the promise land through any other route than the desert? Yes of course! But Israel would have failed woefully to learn the lessons that were intended to be learned in the desert with the circumstances that surrounded them. God did all to strip Israel of the arrogance of self-sufficiency, and He still does it today to those He esteems.

## Man's tendency to forsake and forget God

As earlier mentioned, the tendency to be independent from God is a dangerous one, which God is committed to fight against. It may lead you to forsake God and forget Him. When man is satisfied and has all he desires, he usually shifts from God to pursue pleasure and worship self (see Deuteronomy 8: 10-14). God loves you and me too much to allow us choose and pursue the wrong path and He will do all in His power to bring us to depend on Him.

> *"It is the Sovereign LORD who helps me. Who is he that will condemn me? They will all wear out like a garment; the moths will eat them up. Who among you fears the LORD and obeys the word of his servant? Let him who walks in the dark, who has no light, trust in the name of the LORD and rely on his God. But now, all you who light fires and provide yourselves with flaming torches go, walk in the light of your fires and of the torches you have set ablaze. This is what you shall receive from my hand: You will lie down in torment."* (Isaiah 50:9-11)

God wants us to trust in Him and to rely (wholly, completely, totally and perpetually) on Him whether in darkness or in light. More especially when you don't know what to do, instead of turning to your own schemes, turn and rely on your God. Any attempt to do things your own way will only lead to torments and further pain. Do not provide *"a torch"* for yourself, do not *"light your own fire"*. Turn to your God.

When we forsake God we sin, and when we try to do things independent of Him we sin further. Is that not why He said, "…my people have committed two sins. They have forsaken me, the spring of living water, and have dug their own cisterns, broken cisterns that cannot hold water." (Jer 2: 13). First there is the forsaking, then there is substituting, these make it double sinning.

Again He asked,

> *"Have you not brought this on yourselves by forsaking the LORD your God when he led you in the way? Now why go to Egypt to drink water from the Shihor? And why go to Assyria to drink water from the River? Your wickedness will punish you; your backsliding will rebuke you. Consider then and realize how evil and bitter it is for you when you forsake the LORD your God and have no awe of me, "declares the Lord, the LORD Almighty."* (Jeremiah 2:17-19).

## He did it to Samson

> *"As he approached Lehi, the Philistines came toward him shouting. The Spirit of the LORD came upon him in power. The ropes on his arms became like charred flax, and the bindings dropped from his hands. Finding a fresh jawbone of a donkey, he grabbed it and struck down a thousand men. Then Samson said, "With a donkey's jawbone I have made donkeys of them. With a donkey's jawbone I have killed a thousand men." When he finished speaking, he threw away the jawbone; and the place was called Ramath Lehi. Because he was very thirsty, he cried out to the LORD, "You have given your servant this great victory. Must I now die of thirst and fall into the hands of the uncircumcised?" Then God opened up the hollow place in Lehi, and water came out of it. When Samson drank, his strength returned and he revived. So the spring was called En Hakkore, and it is still there in Lehi."* (Judges 15:14-19)

Here we find a perfect example of how God teaches His children to depend on Him. After such a great victory, the tendency was for Samson to delight in his victory over the Philistines and shift his focus from God. Samson's statement shows that he gave the glory to himself and his weapon. No praise was given to God in that victory declaration. The donkey's jawbone appears twice and *"I have"* also appears twice as though the strength came from him and the jawbone. God had to draw Samson's attention once more from his victory, himself and his weapon to Him (God). So He caused Samson to thirst in a place where there was no ready source of water. His jawbone could not satisfy his thirst though it had given him victory over a thousand men. Besides, he had thrown it away.

The truth is that whatever you may want to depend on cannot work in all situations. The arm of flesh will always be limited in the extent to which it may provide help. Only God is all-sufficient to solve every puzzle of life. No matter how sophisticated any other weapon may be it surely will fail. Samson's thirst pushed him to turn again to God in total dependence. It is only during this desperate thirst that Samson acknowledged that God was the One who had given him victory over the Philistines. His desperation led him to acknowledge his dependence on God and Him only. He saw no other source of water. If God did not act miraculously, Samson would have been defeated by the Philistines, and for sure God responded. Have you reached a place where you can do nothing but desperately call on God? Where your eyes turn to no one else but Him? If not be sure that He will lead you to such a point. You can trust Him to do it.

When Samson drank from the *"well of God's provision"*, *"his strength returned and he was revived"*. Do you want to regain that which you have lost in the battle of life? Do you want to revive your zeal? Then look up to Him who sits on the throne.

### He did it two three Kings

> *"So the king of Israel set out with the king of Judah and the king of Edom. After a roundabout march of seven days, the army had no more water for themselves or for the animals with them. "What!" exclaimed the king of Israel. "Has the LORD called us three kings together only to hand us over to Moab?" But Jehoshaphat asked, "Is there no prophet of the LORD here,*

> *that we may inquire of the LORD through him?" An officer of the king of Israel answered, "Elisha son of Shaphat is here. He used to pour water on the hands of Elijah." Jehoshaphat said, "The word of the LORD is with him." So the king of Israel and Jehoshaphat and the king of Edom went down to him. Elisha said to the king of Israel, "What do we have to do with each other? Go to the prophets of your father and the prophets of your mother." "No," the king of Israel answered, "because it was the LORD who called us three kings together to hand us over to Moab." Elisha said, "As surely as the LORD Almighty lives, whom I serve, if I did not have respect for the presence of Jehoshaphat king of Judah, I would not look at you or even notice you. But now bring me a harpist." While the harpist was playing, the hand of the LORD came upon Elisha and he said, "This is what the LORD says: Make this valley full of ditches. For this is what the LORD says: You will see neither wind nor rain, yet this valley will be filled with water, and you, your cattle and your other animals will drink. This is an easy thing in the eyes of the LORD; he will also hand Moab over to you. You will overthrow every fortified city and every major town. You will cut down every good tree, stop up all the springs, and ruin every good field with stones"* (2 Kings 3:9-19).

Here we find three kings (the king of Israel, the king of Judah and the king of Edom) forming an alliance to launch an attack on Moab that just rebelled against Israel. Joram never sought God's favor because, of course, he was a descendant of the late king Ahab, an idolater. All he depended on was the might of his alliance with two other kingdoms. He had the full support of the righteous king Jehoshaphat who put at his disposal his arsenal, Calvary and soldiers.

God in His sovereignty knows how to bring the proud and haughty to their knees. He can always create circumstances to bring the independent to a corner where their insufficiency is exposed. He can always bring us to a point where we see ourselves totally useless and incapacitated without Him. The sad thing is that many, too many, are too slow in learning this simple reality; that man can do nothing, absolutely nothing that will last or endure adverse conditions, without God. Many are bent on learning it the hard way.

How many of God's children depend totally on their alliances with the apparent might of the world's financial institutions? How many depend on the *"security"* these institutions offer? A time will come, and is already at hand when those who pledge true allegiance to the King of the universe and to His Christ will have no place in these systems.

Certainly God did not gather these three kings to hand them over to Moab as the king of Israel insinuated. He gathered them to let them know in spite of the might of their army, cavalry and arsenal, the outcome of the battle is determined by Him. He wanted them to know man can never and will never be independent of God. He wanted them to see their limitation as far as controlling the activities of nature is concerned.

In spite of America's military might and technological advancements, they could do nothing to stop the damage caused by the hurricanes Rita and Katrina. Man can never and will never get nature under his control in spite of how he tries. And God will use the forces of nature to bring us down the lofty heights of our technological advancements.

Notice that it is only after their failure to find water in the helpless situation in which they found themselves that they decided to inquire of the Lord.

Do not wait until the situation gets too bad before you acknowledge God. Do not let it be too late before you set out to inquire of the Lord.

Now the primary lesson I want you to learn from this section is that God has raised people in the church to speak His word into your life, words that will change situations. Such was Elisha to these three desperate kings. Have you identified in your nation your city, your church etc those whom God has raised and anointed to speak and reverse situations? Elisha spoke the Word of the Lord to these kings so as to bring a solution to their problem.

Have you ever asked a man of God to speak to your circumstances? There are people who God can use to turn around the direction of your tides. Do not remain in your tight corner and let the conditions deteriorate. These kings did not wait until their soldiers and animals started dying of thirst. They decided to act fast before a total disaster stroke, after their fruitless search for a natural source of water.

There are times God will lead us into situations so as to have us experience the supernatural. Yeah! There are situations where the natural conditions may be lacking, but He causes things to happen supernaturally. He told them they would see neither wind nor rain and yet there will be abundance of water. The natural was absent so God would reveal to them the supernatural. God is not a respecter of persons. Those who believe His prophets will succeed in life. It is true that there are too many false prophets out there claiming to pledge allegiance to the Lamb and people truly do not know what to believe. You need to watch, pray and discern. Find out if the person's words and life are consistent with each other and above all with the written word of God.

> *"Early in the morning they left for the Desert of Tekoa. As they set out, Jehoshaphat stood and said, "Listen to me, Judah and people of Jerusalem! Have faith in the LORD your God and you will be upheld; have faith in his prophets and you will be successful."* (2 Chronicles 20:20).

Thus, when all seems fading seek the word from the Lord or through a prophet of His. It is true that we all as children of God have the mandate to inquire of God. He has promised to answer and reveal things to us. But some people are more mature to hear what He is saying or read signs of what He is showing. Others have a special anointing to address the storms of life and command them. There are people who can arrest the circumstances troubling your life, after all God raised them up for that very reason. However, your eyes must look up to God; allow Him to lead you to the place of your solution.

# CHAPTER 17

## Your Reward Shall Come

---

Many times, when things are not moving the way we think they should, the tendency is for us to try to give up the effort of investment for fear that the reward won't come. If there is any principle of the Kingdom I'm so sure of, it is the *"sow and reap principle"*. Everyone shall receive a reward for whatever is done for the sake of His Kingdom.

> *"Anyone who receives a prophet because he is a prophet will receive a prophet's reward, and anyone who receives a righteous man because he is a righteous man will receive a righteous man's reward. And if anyone gives even a cup of cold water to one of these little ones because he is my disciple, I tell you the truth, he will certainly not lose his reward."* (Matthew 10: 41-42).

For all that you do, God will reward you. Even though things seem fading, hold on to what you have been doing. The Bible says, *"let us not become weary in doing good, for at the proper time we will reap a harvest if we do not give up."* (Galatians 6:9) When will the harvest come? At the proper time! Under what condition? If we do not give up!

You see, giving up disqualifies us from the reward (harvest). Let us press on even in the face of adversity to do that which must be done.

## God does not forget

> *"For God is not unfair. How can he forget your hard work for him, or forget the way you used to show your love for him- and still do - by helping his children? And we are anxious that you keep right on loving others as long as life lasts, so that you will have your full reward. Then, knowing what lies ahead of you, you won't become spiritually dull and indifferent, but you will be anxious to follow the example of those who receive all that God has promised them because of their strong faith and patience.* (Hebrew 6:10-12, Living Bible).

For how long have you worked without having the anticipated reward? The truth is that God is not unfair to forget that which you so whole-heartedly do for Him. He cannot forget your hard work and your investments. He cannot forget your patience and your perseverance. He cannot forget your sacrifices on behalf of the Gospel and the Kingdom. He cannot forget your love shown Him as you have reached out to the lost sheep. God cannot forget your labors to put food within the reach of His children. Faithfulness is the only sure guarantee of a full reward. Does He not say: *"But as for you, be strong and do not give up, for your work will be rewarded"* (2 Chronicles 15:7).

As for you who do His will, as for you who are pursuing your calling, as for you who are working towards your calling in spite of the opposition.

> In spite of the pain,
> In spite of the suffering,
> In spite of the apparent defeat and failure;

Be strong in the Lord and do not give up because your work will be rewarded. This is His promise!

> *"Tell the righteous it will be well with them, for they will enjoy the fruit of their deeds."* (Isaiah 3:10)

Your Reward Shall Come

I am announcing to you that it shall be well with you.
It shall be well with your health
It shall be well with your finances
It shall be well with your job
It shall be well with your spirit
It shall be well with your soul
You will enjoy the fruits of your prayers,
You will enjoy the fruits of your worship,
You will enjoy the fruits of your giving,
You will enjoy the fruits of your generosity
You will enjoy the fruit of your Bible reading
You will enjoy the fruit of your service
You will enjoy the fruit of your acts of righteousness
That is the word of the Lord to you, believe it!

## It happened to Mordecai

*"During the time Mordecai was sitting at the king's gate, Bigthana and Teresh, two of the king's officers who guarded the doorway, became angry and conspired to assassinate King Xerxes. But Mordecai found out about the plot and told Queen Esther, who in turn reported it to the king, giving credit to Mordecai. And when the report was investigated and found to be true, the two officials were hanged on a gallows. All this was recorded in the book of the annals in the presence of the king."* (Esther 2:21-23)

*"That night the king could not sleep; so he ordered the book of the chronicles, the record of his reign, to be brought in and read to him. It was found recorded there that Mordecai had exposed Bigthana and Teresh, two of the king's officers who guarded the doorway, who had conspired to assassinate King Xerxes. "What honor and recognition has Mordecai received for this?" the king asked. "Nothing has been done for him," his attendants answered… "Go at once," the king commanded Haman. "Get the robe and the horse and do just as you have suggested for Mordecai the Jew, who sits at the king's gate. Do not neglect anything you have recommended." So Haman got the robe and the horse. He robed Mordecai, and led him on horseback through the*

city streets, proclaiming before him, "This is what is done for the man the king delights to honor!" (Esther 6:1-11)

In the first passage we find Mordecai performing an act of righteousness. He risked it for the king by revealing the plot of these conspirators. In doing this, he knew the consequences should they find out before his message got to the king for him to act on. One would have expected the king to reward Mordecai immediately the investigation was completed but it did not happen that way. The Bible says, *"All this was recorded in the book of the annals in the presence of the king."*

There are things in your favor in the records of the King of the universe. You may think He hasn't taken note of your toils, your sufferings, your pains, the risks you've taken for the sake of the King and the Kingdom and for righteousness; but all are in the books. The truth is that God keeps records of our good deeds and investments in the lives of others and in the Kingdom than we are aware of. Every act of kindness and of justice and of righteousness is recorded by the angels in charge of records in the very presence of the King of the ages.

There are three qualities which we all need to ensure we possess so that we reap the rewards for that which we do in His Kingdom:

### 1. Consistence:

The things we do must be in line with divine principles. Our actions should not cancel the effect of each other. If we are to show kindness, which we should, our acts of kindness should be consistent. We must be consisted in acts of righteousness; we must be consistent in our relationship with the King; in loyalty and obedience. Had Mordecai been *"on the wrong side of the bridge"* with respect to his relationship with the king, then he certainly would have lost his reward.

### 2. Persistence:

We must continue to do that which we are doing as long as it is necessary. Many of us give up way too soon. Persistence is another quality which we must possess if we are to reap our rewards in due time. So keep holding on to your dreams even in the face of opposition. Be persistent in your actions and resolves. Remember, God is looking for men and women, boys and girls who have been tested and approved. It takes persistence to go through tests.

### 3. Prevalence:

By prevalence here, I refer to the need to be effective / efficacious in our actions. You know, someone can be consistent and persistent in his actions without being effective and efficacious. The Bible even talks of prayer being *"powerful and effective"* (James 5:16). Thus, it does not suffice to pray but we must ensure that our prayers are effective.

In all you do, go in for effectiveness and efficiency. That will give your actions weight to stand the storms that follow.

In the second passage, when *"the time for Mordecai's reward"* came, nothing could stop him from receiving that which was due him. There was no date scheduled for his reward to be granted but it came anyway. There comes a time when those who are to be the channels of your reward will find it uneasy in every area of their life until you have received your reward. There comes a time when the King of the universe *"will lack sleep"* until He has checked the records to reward you according to what is recorded. God keeps our rewards to pour them upon us when we need them most. He stores them up for the appropriate time to put our enemies to shame.

When God decides to give you honor and recognition, nothing can stop it from coming. Be faithful at the gate where you have been placed and the King will soon get you into the courts and right to the throne-room. Until now, Mordecai had been going on foot, but at the time of reward he had to ride on a horse with a personal driver. Mordecai who had been putting on sackcloth was now given a royal robe to put on. In the split of a second, the King of the universe, if it is in His will for you, can take you from peasantry to royalty, from insignificance to notoriety, from obscurity to prominence, from dishonor to honor.

The very people who have sought your ruin will be commanded by the King to cloth you and ride you on royalty.

>    Do you want the tables turned?
>    Do you want the tides reversed?

Then be consistent, persistent and prevalent.

# CHAPTER 18

## Twenty Things that will Make or Mar your Destiny

To conclude this trilogy, let us look at some very important points which have the potentials to make or mar your destiny.

**Your Attitudes:**

Our attitudes affect us in almost all areas of life far more than we think. Attitudes towards different aspects can make or mar the destiny of a man or woman.

1. **Your attitudes toward sin:**

The greatest enemy to a man's vision is sin as described in God's word. Sin when committed can be pardoned but its consequences cannot be reverted. Throughout scripture, you'll find a number of people whose destiny was permanently marred because of a wrong attitude to sin;

Cain committed the sin of murder and had his future permanently marred. He was disqualified from God's eternal program; that is why man's genealogy through Adam is continued through the lineage of Seth and not Cain.

> *"Then the LORD said to Cain, "Why are you angry? Why is your face downcast? If you do what is right, will you not be accepted? But if you do not do what is right, sin is crouching at your door; it desires to have you, but you must master it."* (Genesis 4: 6, 7)

Sin gets its power through acts of disobedience with one goal, to have mastery over the individual and then destroy him. May I say it on a more serious note:

Sin disqualifies a man from God's purposes. Sin cherished, sin deliberately committed can mar your destiny. God placed the mark of grace on Cain but he however remained a restless wanderer. His destiny was permanently ruined and his inheritance as the first son was transferred to Seth.

Reuben committed the sin of fornication with one of his father's wife and was demoted. His rights as the firstborn were transferred to Joseph.

On the other hand, Daniel and his peers refused to compromise even in a foreign land and God enabled them fulfil their destiny.

Joseph refused to commit the sin of adultery with his master's wife and God elevated him.

Your attitude towards sin can make your destiny if it is godly or mar your destiny if it is ungodly.

2. **Your attitude towards success:**

What is your yardstick with respect to success? Where does your attention go to when you are successful? Success can be a stepping stone to our destiny or a stumbling block depending on how it is handled or regarded. If you pursue success as the world regards success to be, it can lead to greed and unholy discontentment. Sometimes, successes of the past can obstruct your clear view of the failures and shortcomings of the present, which need to be faced and corrected. It can cause you to lose sight of the future.

A positive attitude will be to celebrate success without losing sight of the needs of the present and working towards future challenges.

### 3. Your attitude towards failure:

Nobody ever plans to fail, or maybe I have not just seen one yet. However, there is no life without at least one failure. What matters most is not that a man or woman fails but how he or she regards failure. Like success, failure can be a stepping-stone or a stumbling block depending on one's attitude towards it.

The Bible says *"for though a righteous man falls seven times, he rises again, but the wicked are brought down by calamity."* (Proverbs 24:16).

Why does he rise again and again? Because he knows no failure is final. If you give up easily after a failure, there is no way you can fulfil your destiny.

Every failure is an opportunity to do it a little bit better next time around. It is an opportunity to take your eyes off yourself and *"look up to the hills from where your help comes"*. Unless you build up such a positive attitude towards failure, then there will be every reason to despair and get stuck when failure strikes. You can use your failure to draw valuable lessons for living.

### 4. You attitude towards Praise and Fame:

Praise received can be a source of encouragement or a cause to take pride in oneself. Fame, even when God-given can be a source of ruin. Remember the king Uzziah. Do not allow your mind to dwell on the praises you receive, focus on the grace of God, which enables you to do that which you are doing. Remember Herod who delighted in the praise he received and what befell him. Let us shift the focus from self to God each time there is the temptation to delight in praise. Praise can be the gateway to Pride, Presumption and Prejudice. On the other hand, praise can lead to self-abasement and self-effacement. It all depends on your attitude towards praise. The Lord had a right attitude towards praise even while He was here on earth such that not even all the praises lavished on him by the spies from the Pharisees could get Him trapped by what He said. Refuse to allow your mind to dwell or continuously meditate on praise received.

### 5. Your attitude towards suffering:

If a man knows that God is in control no matter what happens his attitude towards suffering will be a lot different.

> *"Therefore, since Christ suffered in his body, arm yourselves also with the same attitude, because he who has suffered in his body is done with sin. As a result, he does not live the rest of his earthly life for evil human desires, but rather for the will of God."* (1 Peter 4:1-2).

The right attitude towards suffering gets you to focus on the will of God rather than on self and earthly desire. A negative attitude towards suffering can get you centred around yourself and therefore miss your purpose which is always beyond puny self.

### 6. Your attitude towards those in need:

We all need God's favor in order to fulfill our destinies. God's favor to us can be greatly affected by our attitudes to those around us who are in need. A positive attitude to helping others in need can set God working in your favor.

In fact God commands us to maintain a good attitude of open-handedness towards those in need, *"There will always be poor people in the land. Therefore I command you to be open-handed toward your brothers and toward the poor and needy in your land."* (Deuteronomy 15:11).

It is a sin to despise those in need and a total blessing to show kindness.

> *"He who despises his neighbor sins, but blessed is he who is kind to the needy."* (Proverbs 14:21)

> "*He who oppresses the poor shows contempt for their Maker, but whoever is kind to the needy honors God.*" (Proverbs 14: 31).

## 7. Your attitude towards Strangers:

> *"Do not forget to entertain strangers, for by so doing some people have entertained angels without knowing it"* (Hebrews 13: 2).

God at times sends angels in disguise to us on the road to destiny land. Our attitude to them can win their favor or shut them out. Do you remember Abraham, how he welcomed the angels? It is after he entertained those strangers that he was promised a son. What about Lot? It is after he entertained the two strangers that he was rescued from the judgment that was to befall the city. Angels come in the form of strangers; if you have a welcoming attitude and make room for strangers you will be making room for blessings. Do you remember the widow at Zarephath? She welcomed Elijah when she was meeting him for the first time and received the miracle of provision and later on having her son raised form the dead?

What about the Shunammite? She welcomed Elisha and prepared a place for him, offering him food as regularly as he stopped by, and she received her miracle of a son.

> Have a welcoming attitude towards strangers.

## 8. Your attitude towards hurts:

Hurts are emotional wounds inflicted on us by fellow humans deliberately or mistakenly. An unforgiving and revengeful attitude makes you vulnerable, ineffective and consequently unproductive. Keeping an unforgiving attitude only deepens the wound and makes it difficult to be healed. Also a wrong attitude towards hurts can deprive you of the forgiveness you so badly need, daily from the Lord.

> "*For if you forgive men when they sin against you, your heavenly Father will also forgive you. But if you do not forgive men their sins, your Father will not forgive your sins.*" (Matthew 6:14-15)

A wrong attitude towards hurts can limit your view of the potentials and goodness of others, causing you to shut them out of your world. Hurts can make you to become an Island amongst people, looking at everyone with suspicion and resentment. When this happens, a man's social life is in chaos, which leads to emotional breakdown and depression.

On the other hand, an attitude of forgiveness and reconciliation can go a long way to maintaining relationships and allowing God to use these hurts to accomplish His will for your life.

9. **Your attitude towards rebuke and correction:**

   *"A man who remains stiff-necked after many rebukes will suddenly be destroyed--without remedy."* (Proverbs 29:1).

   *"At the end of your life you will groan, when your flesh and body are spent. You will say, "How I hated discipline! How my heart spurned correction! I would not obey my teachers or listen to my instructors. I have come to the brink of utter ruin in the midst of the whole assembly." Drink water from your own cistern, running water from your own well."* (Proverbs 5:11-14).

A negative attitude towards rebuke and correction can mar one's destiny permanently. The Bible says continuously despising or hating rebukes brings a man to destruction without remedy. The Bible says it will be a sudden destruction, in other words it will not be obvious that destruction is coming until it has happened. Let me ask you a personal question, what is your attitude towards rebuke?

Despising correction does not bring immediate setbacks but in the long run it is devastating when you look back and regret without remedy for having kept a wrong attitude towards correction.

On the other hand, a right attitude towards correction makes a man's destiny.

> *"He who ignores discipline comes to poverty and shame, but whoever heeds correction is honored."* (Proverbs 13:18)

> *"He who ignores discipline despises himself, but whoever heeds correction gains understanding."* (Proverbs 15:32).

A good attitude towards correction brings you honor and keeps you from poverty and ruin and gives you a better understanding of the puzzles in life.

## 10. Your attitude towards God's Word:

God has given us His word, as a guide to enable us live effective and fruitful lives. Your attitude to His word determines how you conduct your daily affairs, both at home and at work. We live in a generation where people want to choose what to obey in God's revealed word. The Bible says, *"You have laid down precepts that are to be fully obeyed"* (Psalm 119: 4).

God's word is to be fully obeyed, not rationalized. Regard it as absolute in your life. The effectiveness of your life depends on your attitude towards the word of God.

> *"Be strong and very courageous. Be careful to obey all the law my servant Moses gave you; do not turn from it to the right or to the left, that you may be successful wherever you go. Do not let this Book of the Law depart from your mouth; meditate on it day and night, so that you may be careful to do everything written in it. Then you will be prosperous and successful."* (Joshua 1:7-8).

Your success depends on how much value you give to the word of God.

Your prosperity depends on how much value you give to the word of God.

Allow the word of God to determine what you approve and disapprove.

### 11. Your attitude towards messengers of God:

In this generation where *"everyone does as he wishes"*, where messengers of God are despised especially when they bring messages of warning and judgment, the one who maintains an attitude of respect to today's prophets will heed God's warning.

You cannot separate your attitude towards God from your attitude towards His servants. The Lord Jesus said to the seventy-two when He sent them out to preach the Word, *"He who listens to you listens to me; he who rejects you rejects me; but he who rejects me rejects Him who sent me."* (Luke 10:16).

> *"All the people, even the tax collectors, when they heard Jesus' words, acknowledged that God's way was right, because they had been baptized by John. But the Pharisees and experts in the law rejected God's purpose for themselves, because they had not been baptized by John"* (Luke 7:29-30).

Do you see that? The Pharisees and experts in the law rejected God's purpose for themselves by putting up a wrong attitude towards John. God identifies Himself totally with His messengers irrespective of their weaknesses.

What is your attitude towards your Pastor and other people God uses to speak His word to you?

Do you think you can separate your attitude to God's servant from your attitude to God?

A good heart attitude towards God's messengers will make your destiny.

> *"He who receives you receives me, and he who receives me receives the one who sent me. Anyone who receives a prophet because he is a prophet will receive a prophet's reward, and anyone who receives a righteous man because he is a righteous man will receive a righteous man's reward. And if anyone gives even a cup of cold water to one of these little ones because he is my disciple, I tell you the truth, he will certainly not lose his reward"* (Matthew 10:40-42).

## 12. Last and most important, your attitude towards God:

Your attitude towards God leads you to a position of independence from Him or to a position of total dependence on Him. Many people see God as an intruder to their life and plans such that they do everything to keep Him out of their lives, reason for the many wrecks and broken hearts and lives.

> *"The vision concerning Judah and Jerusalem that Isaiah son of Amoz saw during the reigns of Uzziah, Jotham, Ahaz and Hezekiah, kings of Judah. Hear, O heavens! Listen, O earth! For the LORD has spoken: "I reared children and brought them up, but they have rebelled against me. The ox knows his master, the donkey his owner's manger, but Israel does not know, my people do not understand." Ah, sinful nation, a people loaded with guilt, a brood of evildoers, children given to corruption! They have forsaken the LORD; they have spurned the Holy One of Israel and turned their backs on him. Why should you be beaten anymore? Why do you persist in rebellion? Your whole head is injured, your whole heart afflicted. From the sole of your foot to the top of your head there is no soundness-- only wounds and welts and open sores, not cleansed or bandaged or soothed with oil."* (Isaiah 1:1-6)

God wants nothing but the best for you. Maintaining an attitude of independence only leads to failure and ruin.

> *"In his heart a man plans his course, but the LORD determines his steps"* (Proverbs 16:9).

> *"Many are the plans in a man's heart, but it is the LORD's purpose that prevails"* (Proverbs 19:21).

The truth is that the universe is God's and He has the sovereign right to determine what happens in this world, in general and in your life in particular. Nothing but failure and defeat awaits the man who sees God as an intruder.

On the other hand, if you make Him Lord of your life and resolve to live in absolute dependence on Him, you will go a long way to succeed.

> *"Commit to the LORD whatever you do, and your plans will succeed"* (Proverbs 16:3).

Do you see that? Whatever you do? You only need to commit it to God's hand and success is guaranteed. To commit means to put Him in charge, absolute charge.

Again the Bible says

> *"Trust in the LORD with all your heart and lean not on your own understanding; in all your ways acknowledge him, and he will make your paths straight"* (Proverbs 3:5-6).

Do not lean on your human wisdom, do not lean on your past successes, but trust in God and depend on Him and He will surely guide and direct your destiny.

You need to transform your thinking and change your attitude for the better,

> *"You were taught, with regard to your former way of life, to put off your old self, which is being corrupted by its deceitful desires; to be made new in the attitude of your minds"* (Ephesians 4: 22-23).

Only this transformation will give you a right attitude towards all we have mentioned here and most especially towards God and His will for your life.

> *"Do not conform any longer to the pattern of this world, but be transformed by the renewing of your mind. Then you will be able to test and approve what God's will is--his good, pleasing and perfect will"* (Romans 12:2).

God's will for you will be viewed as good, pleasing and perfect only after the transformation of your attitude.

**Your Actions:**

By actions, I refer here to acts of volition; the things you choose to do with your time, money and other resources. Your actions can make or mar your destiny.

The things you do are like seeds sown which will bring forth fruit in due season.

### 1. Whatever you sow, that shall you reap

> "*Do not be deceived: God cannot be mocked. A man reaps what he sows*" (Galatians 6:7).

This is a moral law governing God's universe. What you sow determines what you reap and depending on the kind of soil, you surely will reap fruits in different degrees of abundance.

> "*The one who sows to please his sinful nature, from that nature will reap destruction*" (Galatians 6:8a).

Acts of sin, sown to please the sinful nature refers to acts that are contrary to God's moral laws. Such actions bring forth nothing but destruction (of the destiny and potentials) of the one involved.

> "*I have observed those who plough evil and those who sow trouble reap it.*" (Job 4:8).

Some people are experts in ploughing evil i.e. they make the ground ready for others to sow. Here we see that both he who ploughs and he who sows acts of trouble will reap trouble and evil.

On the other hand *"the one who sows to please the Spirit, from the Spirit will reap eternal life"* (Galatians 6: 8b): Your actions in accord with the Spirit's leadership bring you eternal life.

> "*Sow for yourselves righteousness, reap the fruit of unfailing love, and break up your unploughed ground; for it is time to seek the LORD, until he comes and showers righteousness on you*"(Hosea 10:12a).

## 2. Acts of righteousness

You will be the first person to reap from your actions. That is why it says (sow for yourselves), what kind of seed? Righteousness! What is the fruit? Unfailing love with all that comes along with it.

## 3. Acts of Peace

*"Peace makers who sow in peace raise a harvest of righteousness"* (James 3:18). You can also sow in peace. Be a peacemaker, this will greatly influence your destiny for the better.

> *"Let us not become weary in doing good, for at the proper time we will reap a harvest if we do not give up. Therefore, as we have opportunity, let us do good to all people, especially to those who belong to the family of believers"* (Galatians 6:9-10).

## 4. Acts of goodness.

As you do good to others, without giving up, you are storing up for yourself a harvest which will show up at the proper time.

Another thing is sure; our actions do not just determine what we reap in this life but also in the life to come.

The Psalmist said, *"Surely you will reward each person according to what he has done"*.

He understood it clearly and chose his actions wisely.

The LORD of glory said

> *"I will strike her children dead. Then all the churches will know that I am he who searches hearts and minds, and I will repay each of you according to your deeds"* (Revelations 2:23).

> *"Then I heard a voice from heaven say, "Write: Blessed are the dead who die in the Lord from now on." "Yes," says the Spirit, "they will rest from their labor, for their deeds will follow them"* (Revelations 14:13).

Your deeds (actions) determine your reward on the day of rewards and their fruits whether positive or negative will follow you into eternity.

**Your Associations (Affiliations):**

By associations, I mean those with whom you have companionship or partnership consciously or unconsciously. This includes classmates, colleagues, business partners or associates, mentors, counsellors etc.!

One may be deceived to think associations, have no effect on man's destiny; that you can hang around with whomever and decide what to copy from them, forgetting to know that the human brain stores whatever information it receives consciously or unconsciously. Every (group of) person(s) you hang out with, no matter the duration will influence your attitude, values and priorities.

1. **Your associations can make or mar your destiny.**

Let us see what the scripture says about this.

> *"He who walks with the wise grows wise, but a companion of fools suffers harm" (Proverbs 13:20).*

He who walks (make companionship, communes, interacts, stay close to) with wise people will also grow wise. Endeavour to interact with those who possess either natural or experiential wisdom. You will benefit a lot. There is no greater virtue a man needs like wisdom yet it is the virtue no amount of wealth can buy.

> *"He holds victory in store for the upright; he is a shield to those whose walk is blameless, for he guards the course of the just and protects the way of his*

*faithful ones. Then you will understand what is right and just and fair--every good path. For wisdom will enter your heart, and knowledge will be pleasant to your soul. Discretion will protect you, and understanding will guard you. Wisdom will save you from the ways of wicked men, from men whose words are perverse, who leave the straight paths to walk in dark ways, who delight in doing wrong and rejoice in the perverseness of evil, whose paths are crooked and who are devious in their ways. It will save you also from the adulteress, from the wayward wife with her seductive words"* (Proverbs 2:7-16).

*"Get wisdom, get understanding; do not forget my words or swerve from them. Do not forsake wisdom, and she will protect you; love her, and she will watch over you. Wisdom is supreme; therefore get wisdom. Though it cost all you have, get understanding. Esteem her, and she will exalt you; embrace her, and she will honor you. She will set a garland of grace on your head and present you with a crown of splendor"* (Proverbs 4:5-9).

That is what wisdom can do. Do all to associate with men and women, boys and girls of wisdom, and you will surely grow wise.

On the other hand, if you make fools your companions, be sure to suffer harm and ruin. You may ask: "Who is a fool?" Well a fool is one with any of the following characteristics

- One who says there is no God, by words or action (Psalm 14:1);
- One who spreads slander (Proverbs 10:18);
- One who easily gets angry (Proverbs 12: 16);
- Any hot-headed and reckless individual (Proverbs 14:16);
- Anyone who despises his father's discipline (Proverbs 15:5);
- One who fails to listen to others (Proverbs 18:2);
- Any one quick to quarrel (Proverbs 20:3);
- One who trusts in himself (Proverbs 28:26);
- One who refuses to make amends for sin (Proverbs 14:9).

*"Now Lot, who was moving about with Abram, also had flocks and herds and tents. But the land could not support them while they stayed together,*

*for their possessions were so great that they were not able to stay together. And quarreling arose between Abram's herdsmen and the herdsmen of Lot. The Canaanites and Perizzites were also living in the land at that time. So Abram said to Lot, "Let's not have any quarreling between you and me, or between your herdsmen and mine, for we are brothers"* (Genesis 13:5-8).

God had called Abraham (then Abram) and promised to bless him. In obedience Abraham left and Lot went with him. This attachment of Lot to Abraham was a source of Lot's prosperity. The Bible says, *"Lot who was also moving about with Abraham also had flocks and herds and tents."*

Lot's association or companionship with a blessed and prosperous man made him blessed and prosperous.

Who is that blessed man to whom you have ensured a permanent contact?

There are three ways you can keep contact with a blessed and prosperous man. So you too, as an overflow from him, will become blessed and prosperous.

1. Through your hearty service to the person.
2. Through financial or material gifts to the person.
3. Through your prayers and intercessions for the person.

The above do not necessitate a physical contact, because a man can be in physical contact without any spiritual contact.

The moment Lot, through arrogance and greed broke contact with Abraham, his life went down the drain.

*"Then King Rehoboam consulted the elders who had served his father Solomon during his lifetime. "How would you advise me to answer these people?" he asked. They replied, "If today you will be a servant to these people and serve them and give them a favorable answer, they will always be your servants." But Rehoboam rejected the advice the elders gave him and consulted the young men who had grown up with him and were serving him. He asked them, "What is your*

> advice? How should we answer these people who say to me, 'Lighten the yoke your father put on us'?" The young men who had grown up with him replied, "Tell these people who have said to you, 'Your father put a heavy yoke on us, but make our yoke lighter'-tell them, 'My little finger is thicker than my father's waist. My father laid on you a heavy yoke; I will make it even heavier. My father scourged you with whips; I will scourge you with scorpions'" (1 Kings 12:1-11).

Here is a young man who inherited the throne of the world's greatest, wisest and wealthiest king but whose association marred his destiny. In verses 6 and 9 his question to the elders was, *"how will you advise me to answer these people?"* while to the youths who grew up with him asked, *"How should we answer these people..."* The difference is that he dissociated himself from the elders and associated himself with the youths. The pronouns *"you"* and *"we"* clearly portray that Rehoboam identified himself with the wrong people, which brought about his ruin.

> *"Later, Jehoshaphat king of Judah made an alliance with Ahaziah king of Israel, who was guilty of wickedness. He agreed with him to construct a fleet of trading ships. After these were built at Ezion Geber, Eliezer son of Dodavahu of Mareshah prophesied against Jehoshaphat, saying, "Because you have made an alliance with Ahaziah, the LORD will destroy what you have made." The ships were wrecked and were not able to set sail to trade"* (2 Chronicles 20:35-37).

Here is a godly king who decided to get into partnership with a wicked king. His sole purpose was to establish a business, which he hoped, would bring him a great return. God did not take it lightly!

Your associations in business can make or mar your destiny. Do not seek ungodly men for business associates no matter how successful they appear in business, no matter what experience they seem to have gained, no matter how much they want to invest into the venture. Jehoshaphat's investments were brought to ruin because of his association with Ahaziah. Are you business inclined? Choose your business associates not by how much they can put into the business but how much of God they possess.

> "*Amaziah called the people of Judah together and assigned them according to their families to commanders of thousands and commanders of hundreds for all Judah and Benjamin. He then mustered those twenty years old or more and found that there were three hundred thousand men ready for military service, able to handle the spear and shield. He also hired a hundred thousand fighting men from Israel for a hundred talents of silver. But a man of God came to him and said, "O king, these troops from Israel must not march with you, for the LORD is not with Israel--not with any of the people of Ephraim. Even if you go and fight courageously in battle, God will overthrow you before the enemy, for God has the power to help or to overthrow." Amaziah asked the man of God, "But what about the hundred talents I paid for these Israelite troops?" The man of God replied, "The LORD can give you much more than that." So Amaziah dismissed the troops who had come to him from Ephraim and sent them home. They were furious with Judah and left for home in a great rage*" (2 Chronicles 25:5-10).

Your associates can make you vulnerable to defeat and failure. Here we find a king hiring just the wrong kind of people to go into battle with. No matter how courageous he was, no matter the kind of weapons he carried, no matter how much preparation was made, as king he went into battle with the wrong partners and as a result he became vulnerable to defeat and failure. The kind of people you enlist as prayer partners, the kind of people you carry into spiritual warfare can make or mar you.

Ask yourself, whatever or whoever your associates are in whatever domain, about their standing with the God of Heaven. You can lose all you worked for and ruin your business or ministry just because of the wrong associations. King Jehoram's destiny was marred because of his wrong association with the house of Ahab through marriage. His choices, behavior and attitude towards God and the things of God were greatly influenced by his ungodly association.

Your associations are not neutral; they can make or mar your destiny.

**Your Affinities (Attractions):**

Affinities refer to your natural inclinations or drawing; those things which are pleasing or alluring to you. Your affinities can make or mar your destiny. A person's natural inclinations determine a lot about the person.

Your affinities determine your choices:

Choices are not spontaneous decisions. They are determined by a man's inner longings and desires resulting from his heart's inclinations. Your affinities are determined by your desires, which influence your power of choice under any circumstance. Your choice of music, TV programs, literature, conversation topics, etc. is determined by your inclinations. All these things influence your thoughts, opinions, behaviours and actions. If you listen to wild ungodly music, it opens your ears to ungodly stuff and soon your thoughts take the line of the music, your opinions become like those expressed in the music and your behaviour too. If you watch immoral programs over TV, your thoughts become immoral; the desire for immorality gets hold of your mind, your opinion of purity and integrity drops. These are also true of the kind of books you read and the kind of conversations you partake in.

Again your inclinations determine your priorities - things you put top in your agenda with respect to time and money. They determine your expenditure, associations, assets and pursuits. The Psalmist understood it so well that he cried out...

> *"Turn my heart toward your statutes and not toward selfish gain. Turn my eyes away from worthless things; preserve my life according to your word."* (Psalm 119: 36, 37)

He wanted the inclinations of his heart to be towards the statutes of God, such that he could obey His Word and live according to His statutes. He did not allow his affinities to be towards selfish gain. He wanted his eyes to focus on God and not worthless things i.e. God and the things of God should be his attraction and nothing else. James said, *"But each one is tempted when, by his own evil desires, he is dragged away and enticed."* (James 1:14). In other words your inclinations are determined by your inward longings, wishes and desires. The Bible talks of at least seven kinds of desires:

- Sensual desires (1 Timothy 5:11), desires pertaining to physical senses; unduly indulgent to the appetite or sexual pleasure.
- Harmful desires (1 Timothy 6:9); desires inclined towards hurting others or oneself.
- Evil desires (2 Timothy 3:6); desires towards things which generally are morally wrong.
- Sinful desires (1 Peter 2:11); desires which lure you towards things that are against God's written Word.
- Lustful desires (2 Peter 2:18); desires or craving for more of the things the eyes sees especially with respect to materialism.
- Ungodly desires (Jude 18); desires contrary to God's will and nature.
- Covetous desires to own what belongs to others (Romans 7:8).

All the above are the desires of the wicked. Crucify them and like the writer of Hebrews says, desire to live an honorable life (see Hebrews 13:18). That is why the Bible says you should set your heart on things which will take you to where your heart is.

**Your Abilities:**

By abilities, I mean your mental, physical, financial and spiritual capabilities. This includes your natural talents, spiritual gifts and things you have trained yourself to do by necessity, and even acquired knowledge. To improve on your abilities, give yourself to learning and to hard work.

Paul told Timothy, *"Study to shew yourself approved unto God…"* (2 Timothy 2: 15 KJV). If you have to study to gain God's approval, what about that of men?

The Living Bible version says, "Work hard so God can say to you, *"Well done."* Study and hard work go a long way to improve on your abilities.

Companies are looking for men and women of great abilities. It has always been like that and will always continue to be like that. Let us see some examples from scripture.

> "*Then the king ordered Ashpenaz, chief of his court officials, to bring in some of the Israelites from the royal family and the nobility- young men without any physical defect, handsome, showing aptitude for every kind of learning, well informed, quick to understand, and qualified to serve in the king's palace. He was to teach them the language and literature of the Babylonians*" (Daniel 1:3-4)

Here was a vacancy in the palace of the great king Nebuchadnezzar that needed to be filled. Listen to the qualities listed:

- From the royal family
- From the nobility
- Without physical defect
- Handsome
- Showing aptitude for every kind of learning
- Well informed
- Quick to understand
- Qualified to serve in the king's palace.

Of these eight qualities, the first four were natural endowments. However the last four could be acquired through study, hard work, training and discipline. Improve on that which you can do to the fullest capacity.

When King Saul needed a personal "musical-therapist"? What did he require?

> "*It required someone who plays well.*" (1 Samuel 16:17).

> "One of the servants answered, "I have seen a son of Jesse of Bethlehem who knows how to play the harp. He is a brave man and a warrior. He speaks well and is a fine-looking man. And the LORD is with him." (1 Samuel 16:18)

Let us again bring out the list of abilities given here.

- Knows how to play the harp well
- A brave man
- A warrior
- Speaks well
- Find looking
- The LORD is with him.

All the above but one, are acquired abilities. You too can be sought after if you work hard to improve on yourself. Take note that all these qualities we have cited in both passages fall in either the natural, mental or spiritual. There are lots of avenues for you to improve on your abilities in all these domains.

When the Temple was about to be built, the Bible says, *"King Solomon sent to Tyre and brought Huram"* (1 Kings 7:13), who was half-Israelite. Why was he imported from a foreign land? Because of his great skills and abilities!

> *"I am sending you Huram-Abi, a man of great skill, whose mother was from Dan and whose father was from Tyre. He is trained to work in gold and silver, bronze and iron, stone and wood, and with purple and blue and crimson yarn and fine linen. He is experienced in all kinds of engraving and can execute any design given to him. He will work with your craftsmen and with those of my Lord, David your father." (2 Chronicles 2:13-14)*

Huram was a man:

- Of Great skill
- Trained to work
- Experienced.

In this world which is fast becoming a global village, the barriers of race and culture and tribe are being broken and entrepreneurs are looking for those who can offer the best.

On the other hand abilities can be a detriment to an extent. There are people who crave for new abilities and labor to master nothing. It is not how many things a man can do but how well he can do them. Instead of having ten abilities and mastering none, why not have two and a master at least one?

Even in the domain of spiritual abilities you have to train yourself. The gifts you have must be developed to maturity.

> *"But solid food is for the mature, who by constant use have trained themselves to distinguish good from evil."* (Hebrews 5:14)

> *"Our people must learn to devote themselves to doing what is good, in order that they may provide for daily necessities and not live unproductive lives."* (Titus 3:14)

Do you see the words used here? Training and learning.

## Your Assets

By assets I mean the things you (regard as valuable to) have. Your assets are not neutral. They too, influence your destiny in one-way or another. They can propel you along that road to your destiny or weigh you down and render you ineffective. Your assets determine how you spend time, money and other resources. Your assets, to an extent determine which kinds of people are drawn to you for the wrong or right motives. They can determine what value you place on human relationships.

The books in your library are assets; they can make or mar your destiny because they "determine the kind of information which enters your mind".

The audio and videotapes you possess determine the kind of music you listen to and the kind of movie you watch. Your TV set can be helpful for the purpose of information or short-term relaxation but when turned into an object of worship, where you spend most of your time, it can mar your destiny. Your assets determine whether you are a spender or an investor.

Ask yourself daily *"what are the things in my keeping which I do not really need?" "How can this one help me to live an effective life?"*

Attachments to possessions can make you short sighted or lose sight completely of the ultimate purpose in life. The things you possess can make you lose sight of your need for God and other people. The rich young ruler's attachment to his possessions prevented him from following the Lord into his destiny. (See Matthew 19:16-21). Proverbs 11:28 says; *"whoever trust in his riches will fall…"*

**Foresight:**

Foresight refers to thoughtful care or anticipation of the future. In short, foresight is vision. A man's destiny is fulfilled on the basis of whether he is able to possess vision (foresight) or not.

Foresight determines our choices, priorities, associations, behaviors and opinion of life and how we react to circumstances.

> *"Where there is no vision, the people perish: but he that keepeth the law, happy is he"* (Proverbs 29:18 KJV).

Vision has the capacity to keep one holding to the lifeline when all seems fading. Vision empowers and emboldens a man to face life's challenges victoriously. The Lord of Glory had a vision for the salvation of mankind and so could undergo all the pain and suffering because He had in mind the big picture of salvation of the souls of men. While on the cross in response to the mockery of the people He would have come down to prove to the few onlookers that He was the Son of God. But because He had a vision for the whole human race far beyond just that generation, He could endure the scorn and shame.

An alternate translation of the above verse reads, *"Where there is no revelation the people cast off restraint"* (NIV).

Revelation is what brings foresight. So where there's no foresight the people cast off restraint. Why? Because there's nothing at stake! Vision determines your bounds and imposes discipline on the one who possesses her. A man of vision selects what he buys or spends on. He chooses his associations based on the impact upon his vision. Vision influences your affinities. It determines what you do with your *"spare time"*, the kind of places you go to, etc. The possession of foresight will make your destiny; the lack of it will mar your destiny.

## Forbearance:

Forbearance talks of patient endurance. Hence it is actually a combination of two different virtues. It talks of the capacity to sustain pain and suffering while waiting tranquilly for an event.

It is but certain that the pathway to realizing your vision or destiny, as a whole is not an easy road on which to have a roller coaster field trip ride. There will be moments of aloneness, moments of rejection, moments of pain and suffering, moments when it will be as though it were you against the forces of nature. What will keep you in quiet anticipation is forbearance. Without forbearance you will certainly give up the pursuit of your destiny when the climb is so steep.

## Faith:

> *"Now faith is being sure of what we hope for and certain of what we do not see."* (Hebrews 11:1)

Faith is the greatest spiritual virtue an obedient man can possess. God is actually looking for men and women of faith as they walk the path to their destinies.

When God asked Abraham to step out to a strange land, it is faith that brought Abraham to step out boldly on his seemingly obscure road to his destiny.

> *"By faith Abraham, when called to go to a place he would later receive as his inheritance, obeyed and went, even though he did not know where he was going. By faith he made his home in the Promised Land like a stranger in a foreign country; he lived in tents, as did Isaac and Jacob, who were heirs with him of the same promise. For he was looking forward to the city with foundations, whose architect and builder is God."* (Hebrews 11:8-10)

Faith is the lifeline to hold on this slippery path to destiny land. The whole of Hebrews 11 dwells on the heroes of faith, how through faith in God they all made their way to fulfilling their destiny.

Now if you are to fulfil your destiny you must have faith in God. He will fulfil all He ordained for you from before the beginning of time. You must have faith in God who has promised:

> *"I will lead the blind by ways they have not known, along unfamiliar paths I will guide them; I will turn the darkness into light before them and make the rough places smooth. These are the things I will do; I will not forsake them."* (Isaiah 42:16)

This is what God is saying to you:

- He will lead you by ways you have not known;
  This talks of nothing but the path to destiny land. Why is it unknown? Because *"a man cannot discover anything about his future"* (Ecclesiastes 7:14)
- Along unfamiliar paths He will guide you:
  Why is it unfamiliar? Because you have never been there! No one travels that path more than once. It is a one-way traffic.
- He will turn the darkness into light before you:

In times of obscurity, when you don't know which way to turn, when darkness surrounds you and you seem left in obscurity, He has promised to make His light shine to dispel the darkness. He has promised to shine His light of revelation because He says *"where there is no revelation the people cast off restraint,"* (Proverbs 29:18a). He will bring His revelation to keep you in the right path.

- He will make the rough places smooth:
The rough places on the path to your destiny signify failures, weakness, and the difficulties you will meet. He has promised to take care of them. What are the rough places you dread?
God has promised to make them smooth. Go ahead along that path and let Him do that which He has promised.

The Bible says in Luke 5, *"When Jesus saw their faith …"* God is looking for men and women of faith. He is looking for faith in the heart of young men and women, old men and women, boys and girls and why not children?

God responds to nothing but faith! It was faith in the hearts of these people which caused them to surmount the barriers of nature, circumstances and normal protocol to reach the presence of Jesus. Their faith brought about a permanent change in their friend's future as he received his healing from the Master.

Have faith and believe God for all He has promised.

Faith in God can make your destiny and the lack of it can mar your destiny.

Also, when faith steps out of proper bounds, it becomes presumption. There is a wise counsel which reads, *"a prudent man sees danger and takes refuge, but the simple keep going and suffer for it"* (Proverbs 22:3). Avoid turning faith to presumption; this can lead to nothing but destruction. Josiah's faith became presumptuous and led to his premature death. We shall dwell on presumptions later.

**Facts:**

There are moments in life when we just must face facts, the things that are. A wise confrontation with the realities of life will help make your destiny. It is true that *"we live by faith, not by sight."* (2 Corinthians 5:7), and *"…the righteous will live by his faith"* (Hebrews 2:4). Does it mean that we refuse confronting the facts of life? Certainly not! Some people can be very comfortable with a life dreaming, refusing to confront the basic realities. Facts are not meant for you to plan or align your life according to their dictates but to cause you to lift up your eyes to the realm of the supernatural hand of the Almighty, Omnipotent God.

Facts can make or mar your destiny depending on how you view them. For example the king of Assyria came and laid siege against Jerusalem during the reign of king Hezekiah, (See Isaiah 36 and 37). After his many boast and threats, the Bible says *"Hezekiah received the letter from the messengers and read it. Then he went to the temple of the Lord and spread it out before the Lord. And Hezekiah prayed to the Lord: O Lord Almighty, God if Israel, enthroned between the cherubim, you alone are God over all the kingdoms of the earth. You have made heaven and earth. Give ear, O Lord, and hear; open your eyes O Lord and see; listen to all the words Sennacherib has sent to insult the living God. it is true O lord that the Assyrian kings have laid waste all these people and their lands. They have thrown their gods into the fire and destroyed them, for they were not gods but only wood and stone, fashioned by human hands. Now, O Lord our God, deliver us from his hand, so that all kingdoms on earth may know that you alone, O Lord, are God"* (Isaiah 37:14-20).

Hezekiah considered what the Assyrian Kings had done in the past and were still capable of doing. This drove him on his knees in total dependence on his God, and surely victory came for Hezekiah.

Asa was another king who relied on God when under attack and got victory. But at one time the facts drove him to depend on his silver and gold and on the king of Aram, and this brought about his failure.

The twelve spies during the exodus through the wilderness in Numbers 13 and 14 Are also an example. When they left to explore the land, they were a single camp, but after exploring the land, they were now two camps, on the bases of how they faced the facts listed here below.

> "But the people who live there are powerful and the cities are fortified and very large. We even saw descendants of Anak there" (Numbers 13:28).

All twelve faced the same fact; positive and negative. One group responded to the facts negatively by dwelling on their own inabilities and incapacities instead of depending on God. This wrong attitude to the facts disqualified them from entering the Promised Land, which they were destined for.

The other group responded correctly to the facts by turning to the promises of their God and what He could accomplish through them. This attitude caused them to inherit what God had promised hence fulfilled their destiny. Facts can make or mar your destiny depending on how you respond to them.

**Friends:**

When we dealt with the subject of associations, I left out friends because amongst all the non-genetic associations, friendship is the most intimate.

A friend is an intimate and trust worthy companion. We can deal with the other associations like colleagues, mates etc at arm's length. But when it comes to friends, there are the added and indispensable virtues of trustworthiness and intimacy. Friends are the ones you will easily share your desires, delights, difficulties, failures and weaknesses with. Because of this, I want you to know that friendship can make or mar your destiny. The Bible says, "a righteous man is cautious in friendship" (Proverbs 12:13a) Why? Because friends play a very important role in the life of a man or woman! Your friends can promote or ruin you. Exercise prudence in selecting your friends based on their purpose, values, attitudes, likes and dislikes, priorities etc. Do not just allow anyone to enter your circle of friends. Evaluate the grounds for companionship, intimacy, and trustworthiness, before sharing your heart with the person. Do not make haste in making friends. Prayerfully consider who to approach for friendship and whose friendship to validate. Why?

Because *"A man of many companions may come to ruin, but there is a friend who sticks closer than a brother"* (Proverbs 18:24).

A man of many companions may come to ruin, what more of a man of many friends - close companions - not just companions. Heed the warning and be wise in making friends. The Bible says, *"Beware of your friends"* (Jeremiah 9: 4) and *"friends deceive friend, and no one speaks the truth"* (Jeremiah 9: 5).

On a positive note His eternal word says, *"a friend loves at all times…"* (Proverbs 17:7) and *"…there is a friend who sticks closer than a brother"* (Proverbs 8:24b). That is the real value of true friendship, someone who will love you at all times for who you are, someone who will stick closer when everyone else is deserting you. He says; *"a despairing man should have the devotion of his friends, even though he forsakes the fear of the Almighty"* (Job 6:14). You need such people in your life, who will stick close to the end of the road with you. After all *"greater love has no one than this, that He laid down His life for His friends"* (John 15:13). Ask the Lord to lead you in the wise and cautious selection of friends.

People have risen to unexpected heights because of friends and others have come to sudden ruin because of friends. Only the Lord can lead us to choose our friends wisely. You can trust Him.

## Favor:

Favor, when bestowed on a man or woman, boy or girl will make his or her destiny, and the lack of it may mar his or her destiny. Throughout scripture, you find individuals whose situations were changed for the better because they found favor with God and man.

If John the Baptist was right, and I believe he was, then you can only find favor with men if favor has been bestowed on you from Heaven's courts. For He said, *"a man can receive only what is given him from Heaven"* (John 3:27).

To succeed in life, you need both favor with God and favor before man. *"And the boy Samuel continued to grow in stature and in favor with the Lord and with men."* (1 Samuel 2:26) Any doubt Samuel had such a successful ministry in the three fold capacity of priest, prophet and Judge in Israel?

What about the only Begotten, Sovereign and Eternal Son of God? It is written, *"And Jesus grew in wisdom and stature, and in favor with God and men"* (Luke 2: 52). If God's Son needed favor before God and man, then you and I need it more, even more than we know or think. Why was Mary chosen to be the mother of the Savior of Mankind? Because she found favor with the God of creation! (see Luke 1:30).

What took Esther to the throne of the Persian Empire? Nothing but favor!

> *"Now the king was attracted to Esther more than to any of the other women, and she won his favor and approval more than any of the other virgins. So he set a royal crown on her head and made her queen instead of Vashti"* (Esther 2:17).

## How to obtain favor

### 1. Obedience.

Obedience is an open door to favor with man. If you want to find favor, be obedient. Esther's favor before Hegai was certainly due to her obedient attitude from childhood as suggested in verse twenty of chapter two.

Now, the Bible says, *"And this is how she would go to the king: Anything she wanted was given her to take with her from the harem to the king's palace."* (Esther 2:13)

Anyone could ask for whatever she wanted to take into the king's presence in order to win the king's approval. There was freedom of choice according to one's taste.

> *"When the turn came for Esther (the girl Mordecai had adopted, the daughter of his uncle Abihail) to go to the king, she asked for nothing other than what Hegai, the king's eunuch who was in charge of the harem, suggested. And Esther won the favor of everyone who saw her"* (Esther 2:15).

Her obedience to Modecai caused her to find favor with Hegai, and her obedience to Hegai, caused her to find favor with everyone who saw her and subsequently favor with the king. Obedience courts favor more than you can ever imagine (see Leviticus 26).

### 2. Holiness:

Living in holiness and righteousness opens the way for favor from the King of Righteousness. In a world where unrighteousness seems to be on the rise, living holy will cause you to find favor before the God of holiness.

> *"But Noah found favor in the eyes of the LORD. This is the account of Noah. Noah was a righteous man, blameless among the people of his time, and he walked with God"* (Genesis 6:8-9).

Verse 9 gives us the reason why Noah found favor with God.

- He was righteous
- He was blameless
- He walked with God.

Holiness makes way for the favor of God's anointing to rest upon an individual. About the Messiah, it is said,

*"You have loved righteousness and hated wickedness; therefore God, your God, has set you above your companions by anointing you with the oil of joy."* (Hebrews 1:9).

Do you need the favor of God's anointing in your ministry, then be holy, set your heart on righteousness! Even the Psalmist knew this and said, *"For surely, O LORD, you bless the righteous and surround them with your favor as with a shield"* (Psalm 5:12)

### 3. Love and Faithfulness:

*"Let love and faithfulness never leave you; bind them around your neck, write them on the tablet of your heart. Then you will win favor and a good name in the sight of God and man."* (Proverbs 3:3 - 4)

Another gateway into the land of favor with God and with man is to live in love - love towards God and towards man - and to practice faithfulness in whatever your hand finds to do and more so in your duty and calling as a Christian.

### 4. Wisdom:

*"Whoever finds me finds life and receives favor from the LORD."* (Proverbs 8: 35)

As you seek and find wisdom from the LORD, He bestows on you His favor. This is because wisdom will lead you on the path of righteousness and justice. Wisdom will lead you to understand the ways of God and to act with prudence. Go in for wisdom, seek and find wisdom and along with it you will receive God's infinite favor.

### 5. Knowing the ways of the Lord (Exodus 33:13)

See my book *"Fulfilling your destiny"*

6. **Giving**

## What favor does

### 1. Favor will spare you from wrath

> *"But Noah found favor in the eyes of the LORD."* (Genesis 6:8)

At the brink of God's judgment upon renegade humanity, Noah's favor with God caused him and his family to be spared and preserved. That which money or education cannot buy, favor will bring.

### 2. Favor will cause you to behold God's glory

(See Exodus 33:12-23).

Because Moses found favor with God, God was *"forced"* to reveal His glory to him even in the midst of His anger against the children of Israel.

### 3. Favor will cause you to be fruitful

> *"I will look on you with favor and make you fruitful and increase your numbers, and I will keep my covenant with you."* (Leviticus 26:9)

God's favor upon you will make you fruitful in all that you do. Favor brings in a supernatural multiplying factor to your harvest. The secret to financial, spiritual, and biological fruitfulness is to win the Lord's favor.

### 4. Favor will cause your offering to be accepted

> *"But Abel brought fat portions from some of the firstborn of his flock. The LORD looked with favor on Abel and his offering"* (Genesis 4: 4).

> *"Gideon replied, "If now I have found favor in your eyes, give me a sign that it is really you talking to me."* (Judges 6:17).

Our God is a great king, who chooses what to accept from whoever is making the offering. Favor with God will cause Him to accept your offering. Actually it is a privilege to give to Him and it is an honor when He accepts your offerings.

5. **Favor brings Victory.**

> "*It was not by their sword that they won the land, nor did their arm bring them victory; it was your right hand, your arm, and the light of your face, for you loved them*" (Psalm 44:3).

What does *"the light of your face"* signify but God's favor? In this generation where people depend on their strength and weapons, go beyond that to seeking the Lord's favor. That is what brings victory as seen in the Aaronic blessing?

> "*The LORD bless you and keep you; the LORD make his face shine upon you and be gracious to you; the LORD turn his face toward you and give you peace*" (Numbers 6:24-26).

It is nothing but God's favor; making His face to shine upon you and turning His face towards you speak of nothing but His favor.

6. **Favor brings His peace.**

> "*Glory to God in the highest, and on earth, peace to men on whom his favor rests*" (Luke 2:14).

The peace of God is on those who have found favor with Him. The Bible says, God *"gives sleep to those he loves"*. The King James Version translates sleep as rest, and what is there in rest but peace with yourself, with man and above all with God.

Until now, the qualities we have examined above all have a positive and negative side (except favor which is really entirely positive). The next set is actually entirely negative i.e. all they can do is mar your destiny.

## Procrastination:

Procrastination is the habit of delaying action to a later time. If there's one thing that brings poverty, it is the evil of procrastination. It brings spiritual, financial, intellectual, emotional and social poverty.

> *"A sluggard does not plow in season; so at harvest time he looks but finds nothing"* (Proverbs 20:4).

The Bible does not say he did not plough; only that he did not plough in season. Was he unwilling to plough? No! He only deterred the action to a later time, to realize the conditions were no longer favorable for a healthy growth and harvest. The result: Nothing to harvest and consequently poverty. Procrastination is a sin that must be ruthlessly dealt with, for it brings nothing but ruin.

You do not know tomorrow, so what you must do in line with your calling must be done now. Do not postpone it any longer; you might never have the chance.

Some wise men prayed

> *"Show me, O LORD, my life's end and the number of my days; let me know how fleeting is my life. You have made my days a mere handbreadth; the span of my years is as nothing before you. Each man's life is but a breath"* (Psalm 39:4-5).

> *"Teach us to number our days aright, that we may gain a heart of wisdom"* (Psalm 90:12).

How fleeting are those days, how short is the life span. Procrastination robs you of the urgency to live life to the fullest each day. If you understand that your life is but brief, you will endeavor to maximize your days and avoid unreasonable delays. Someone said, *"There is no excuse to be full of excuses"*, think about that! Has not the Word exhorted us to live *"making the most of every opportunity"* (Ephesians 5:16)? For how long will you continue to squander those God-given opportunities for action?

If you learn to number your days, then you will gain a heart of wisdom to live life effectively.

Someone sang,

> *"What is this life but a shadow?*
> *What is this life but a mist?*
> *What is this life but a vapor?*
> *It vanishes away".*

## Pride

Pride is described as an undue sense of one's own superiority or an inordinate self-esteem.

> *"A man's pride brings him low, but a man of lowly spirit gains honor"* (Proverbs 29: 23).

> **"*When pride comes, then comes disgrace, but with humility comes wisdom*"** (Proverbs 11:2).

Pride is another deadly vice anyone can afford to harbor. The only destination of pride is destruction. Pride is the only thing that courts opposition from the Almighty, Omnipotent, Omniscient God. As I said in my book *"Fulfilling your destiny"* under the dangers of pride in service…

As you serve the Lord, be careful not to glory in self. Your promotion can come from your service likewise your disqualification. The Lord is committed to share His glory with no other, not even you.

> *"When the Lord has finished all his work against Mount Zion and Jerusalem, he will say, 'I will punish the king of Assyria for the willful pride of his heart and the haughty look in his eyes. For he says:*
>
> *"'By the strength of my hand I have done this, and by my wisdom, because I have understanding. I removed the boundaries of nations, I plundered their treasures; like a mighty one I subdued their kings'"'* (Isaiah 10:12-13).

When God uses, there's need for self-abasement and self-effacement. God opposes all pride and haughtiness. The Assyrian was a rod in God's hand;

God sent him

God dispatched him.

A man can be called by God, chosen by God, sent by God, for a special purpose, yet God looks at intentions and motives (see Isaiah 10:7). It is a tragedy to go on God's errands with a secret motive and intent. Unless your goal is to do only that for which God sent you, you better not be a part of it.

To whom do you give glory for that which God is using you or for what He has accomplished through you? *God is not only interested in what a man is at the time He is using Him but in what he becomes after God has used him.* You can be greatly used of God today and thrown aside tomorrow if pride and haughtiness come in.

### Presumptuousness:

To be presumptuous means to be unduly confident or bold. Self-confidence can be a virtue in its proper bounds. But when it breaks barriers it becomes inordinate and wild, leading to presumption. Like pride, presumption is something you must labor to eradicate in your life.

> *"The wisdom of the prudent is to give thought to their ways, but the folly of fools is deception"* (Proverbs 14:8).

> *"A simple man believes anything, but a prudent man gives thought to his steps"* (Proverbs 14:15).

Presumption will cause you to refuse to face facts and confront reality. Presumption deafens you to wise counsel and blinds you to truth.

Wisdom demands that you give careful thought and examination to your ways, it will require you sitting down and allowing God to show you who you really are.

Let me take you to the journey of the Israelites in the wilderness, when facts caused a group of spies to rebel against God and His servant, Moses. God gave a verdict and this entailed the people turning to a different direction. The Bible says,

> *"When Moses reported this to all the Israelites, they mourned bitterly. Early the next morning they went up toward the high hill country. "We have sinned," they said. "We will go up to the place the LORD promised." But Moses said, "Why are you disobeying the LORD's command? This will not succeed! Do not go up, because the LORD is not with you. You will be defeated by your enemies, for the Amalekites and Canaanites will face you there. Because you have turned away from the LORD, he will not be with you and you will fall by the sword." Nevertheless, in their presumption they went up toward the high hill country, though neither Moses nor the ark of the LORD's covenant moved from the camp. Then the Amalekites and Canaanites who lived in that hill country came down and attacked them and beat them down all the way to Hormah"* (Numbers 14:39-45).

They presumed that everything will be alright, that they had obtained God's forgiveness, that they were God's people accustomed to victory and so it did not matter whether God's presence went with them or not, whether Moses led the battle or not. What did they meet? Defeat, failure, and death. Many ruined their future by that act of presumption. God help us!

Again the Bible says, *"a prudent man sees danger and take refuge, but the simple keep going and suffer for it"* (Proverbs 22:3).

## Prejudice

By prejudice, we mean opinions or judgments (favorable or unfavorable) formed beforehand without due examination. Prejudice tolerated in your life in any form will mar your destiny. Prejudice can deafen your ears to the cries of the suffering; it can blind your eyes to the needs of those around and even to the working of God in the life of another. You can choose what you believe, but you cannot choose the consequences which follow the belief. It is your responsibility to examine the facts in the light of God's presence.

> *"There is a way that seems right to a man, but in the end it leads to death"* (Proverbs 14:12).

This way is not the right way but just seems right, why? Because there hasn't been any real examination! There're many opinions which just seem right, many actions which just seem right, many relationships which just seem right but due examination will prove the shortcomings. A man who walks the path of prejudice will soon end up in unanticipated ruin and destruction. Remember the Samaritan woman's prejudice against the Jews almost caused her to miss her *"blind date with destiny"."*

> *"The Samaritan woman said to him, "You are a Jew and I am a Samaritan woman. How can you ask me for a drink?" (For Jews do not associate with Samaritans.) Jesus answered her, "If you knew the gift of God and who it is that asks you for a drink, you would have asked him and he would have given you living water." "Sir," the woman said, "you have nothing to draw with and the well is deep. Where can you get this living water? Are you greater than our father Jacob, who gave us the well and drank from it himself, as did also his sons and his flocks and herds?" Jesus answered, "Everyone who drinks this water will be thirsty again, but whoever drinks the water I give him will never thirst. Indeed, the water I give him will become in him*

> a spring of water welling up to eternal life." The woman said to him, "Sir, give me this water so that I won't get thirsty and have to keep coming here to draw water" (John 4:9-15).

There was no greater need this woman had than the Messiah who was standing right before her in this deep-seated conversation yet prejudice almost caused her to miss the day of her visitation. Thank God before the discussion was over her walls of prejudice had crumbled and so the Master could now work in her and through her.

What about the Pharisees? They had a preconception, needless to say it was not founded on the Word of God, of whom the Christ ought to be and where He had to come from. This caused them to label the Messiah who was in the midst as the "false Christ".

> "They replied, "Are you from Galilee, too? Look into it, and you will find that a prophet does not come out of Galilee" (John 7:52).

They were prejudiced against Galilee and hence against all who came from Galilee. This blinded them to the reality of the works the Christ was performing and even to the testimony, which came from heaven when He was baptized and when He raised Lazarus from the dead.

Their prejudice against the tax collectors and others caused them to fail to see the working of God in the lives of these individuals.

I guess someone is saying but all that is because their opinions were all negative i.e. unfavorable, what if my opinions about the person are favorable? Well I tell you as long as it is without due examination, it will mar your destiny.

> "Johanan son of Kareah and all the army officers still in the open country came to Gedaliah at Mizpah and said to him, "Don't you know that Baalis king of the Ammonites has sent Ishmael son of Nethaniah to take your life?" But Gedaliah son of Ahikam did not believe them. Then Johanan son of Kareah said privately to Gedaliah in Mizpah, "Let me go and kill Ishmael

> son of Nethaniah, and no one will know it. Why should he take your life and cause all the Jews who are gathered around you to be scattered and the remnant of Judah to perish?" But Gedaliah son of Ahikam said to Johanan son of Kareah, "Don't do such a thing! What you are saying about Ishmael is not true" (Jeremiah 40:13-16).

It is but clear that if Gedaliah was not prejudiced towards Ishmael he would have carried out thorough investigation of the facts and therefore precautionary measures would have been taken to prevent his eventual murder by Ishmael. His favorable opinion of Ishmael was the sole cause to the success of this plot, which marred his destiny.

Modecai brought a similar report to the king Xerxes but the simple difference is that Xerxes carried out an investigation to examine the reports.

Prejudice can lead to blind trust and the consequences can be far beyond what you think. Does this mean you go about suspecting people? Certainly not! But do not fail to examine the facts when there is need.

## Perfectionism

This is the tendency to demand an extremely high degree of excellence in the performance or behavior of oneself or others.

On the surface this appears to be a virtue but it actually is not. It can lead to undue pressure on oneself. It can cause you to see flaws where there is none and build in you a tendency to concentrate on the negative. It can be very frustrating trying to bring perfection out of the imperfect. Too many people have given up what they were well capable of doing because they looked at it from the point of the imperfections; do not try to take His place. All that matters is for you to do your best.

> *"Do not be over righteous, neither be over wise-- why destroy yourself?"* (Ecclesiates 7:16)

This verse describes nothing but the tendency to be given to perfectionism. Perfectionism can only lead to failure and destruction, avoid it.

## Pessimism:

Pessimism is a disposition to take a gloomy view of affairs. Pessimism is not humility, neither is it dependence upon God. There are some who take the pessimist for the humble. They are anti-parallel lines; one is strength and the other a weakness.

Allow the Spirit of God to build in you confidence. Do not cherish pessimism; it makes you inefficient and purposeless. Don't wait until *"success is guaranteed"* before acting. Do not always look at the shortcomings, failures and weakness; there are a lot more positive things to base your mind on.

Pessimism takes the upper hand over an individual when he or she concentrates on his or her own inabilities. Once your eyes are lifted off your inabilities to God's ability, a new light of hope shines through the *"darkness"*. Abraham's pessimism brought about the existence of Ishmael. Even when God re-iterated the coming of an Isaac, Abraham could only lift his eyes as far as Ishmael and insisted upon God blessing him.

Can you still recall the group of spies who saw themselves as grasshoppers before the Anakites? They concentrated on the negative instead of the positive aspects of the land. Why? Because they looked through the eyes of pessimists! The other group compared the Anakites and their defenses in the light of the strength of the God who was sending them. They saw the positive side of the presence of God. Pessimism will mar your destiny.

## Pleasure:

True hard work and the love of pleasure really do have nothing in common. Anyone given to pleasure lacks real power to concentrate when out of the pleasure zone. The love of pleasure is never a friend to purpose. To fulfil your destiny, avoid the love of pleasure. Have you not read that *"He who* loves pleasure will become poor; whoever loves wine and oil will never be rich" (Proverbs 21:17)?

> If you love pleasure you'll come to spiritual poverty.
> If you love pleasure you'll come to financial poverty.
> If you love pleasure you'll come to intellectual poverty.
> If you love pleasure you'll to material poverty

*"The seed that fell among thorns stand for those who hear, but as they go on their way they are choked by life's worries, riches and **pleasures**, and they do not mature"* (Luke 8:14 emphasis mine).

There is a seed of purpose, which God has planted in each one of us for it to grow into the tree of destiny, where nature, others and yourself can benefit from the harvest. Pleasure is just one of those things which will choke the seed causing it to fail to reach maturity; do you want to fulfil your destiny? Avoid the love of pleasure.

Have you not read already that the love of pleasure and the love of God are on opposite direction on that crossroad with one leading to destiny land and the other to doom land?

(See 2 Timothy 3:4). The passage describes some people as *"lovers of pleasure rather than lovers of God"*, what does it imply? You cannot love God and love pleasure at the same time,

We have come to the end of this section of the negatives,

This next point which actually will be the last is also of dual nature; it can make or mar your destiny.

**Your Proclamations: (pronouncements)**

Proclamations are the things you declare, words which come out of your mouth even when off guard. They can make or mar your destiny. Our words affect us far more than we think.

Why? Because God takes our pronouncements seriously! Did He not say *"As surly as I live, declares the Lord, I will do to you the very things I hear you say"* (Numbers 14:28).

1. Your proclamations can win you favor: *"from the fruit of his lips a man enjoys good things"* (Proverbs 13:29).
   If you want to enjoy the good things in life, speak good.
2. Your proclamations can protect you.
3. Your proclamation can acquit you.
   Our adversary is also called the accuser if the saints before the Judge of the universe. What you declare; the words that come out of your mouth will acquit you.
4. Your Proclamations can provide for you.
   *"From the fruit of his mouth a man's stomach is filled; with the harvest from his lips he is satisfied"* (Proverbs 18:20).
   Many people earn their living by what they allow to come out of their lips: singers, journalists, teachers, preachers etc. The words you speak can fend for you. You can speak words of counsel and wisdom, words of encouragement. Your words can fend for you. On the other hand, your proclamations can mar your destiny.
5. Your proclamations can condemn you.
   *"By your words you will be acquitted, and by your words you will be condemned"* (Matthew 12:37).
   God will hold you accountable for every word ever spoken. Words that violate His moral laws and principles will surely bring about condemnation.
6. Your proclamations can destroy you.
   *"He who guards his lips guards his life, but he who speaks rashly will come to ruin."* (Proverbs 13:3).

7. Your proclamations can defile you.
   *"What goes into a man's mouth does not make him 'unclean,' but what comes out of his mouth, that is what makes him 'unclean.'"*
   (Matthew 15:11).
   Remember we said holiness brings favor. When you are defiled, you block the way to the favor you need so much.
   From the above twenty points, you see that your destiny actually lies on two things; your heart and your mind. The things you allow to get hold of your heart or your mind will greatly influence you. That's why the Bible exhorts us to be renewed in the attitude of our minds and to guard our hearts.
   *"Above all else, guard your hearts, for it is the well spring of life"*
   (Proverbs 4:23).
   Your proclamations will flow from that which is stored up in the heart, *"for out of the overflow of the heart the mouth speaks"*
   (Matthew 12:34).

# In Closing

As Christians, our ultimate commitment must be to please the Lord whatever we are going through. Once you set your heart on glorifying Him through any circumstance, adversity becomes a bridge to intimacy; obstacles become stepping stones to opportunity. I hope you have been blessed and encouraged while going through the pages of this book. If so let us know. We will be glad to help you live victoriously. If you will like to support our book ministry or to order more of our materials, then write to

> E. C. Nakeli
> CMFI
> 40 S church street,
> Westminster, MD 21157
> USA.

# Other publications from the publisher

# Other publications from the publisher

# Other publications from the publisher

Other publications from the publisher

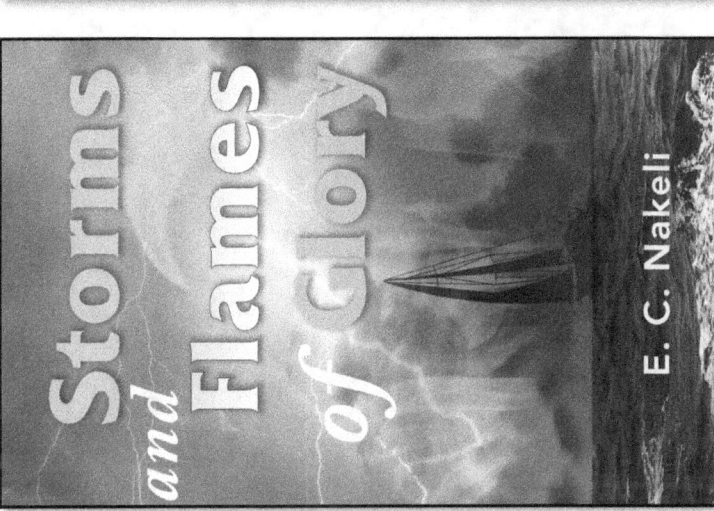

www.ingramcontent.com/pod-product-compliance
Lightning Source LLC
Chambersburg PA
CBHW071625080526
44588CB00010B/1269